I STILL BELIEVE IN TOMORROW

Mike Patrick

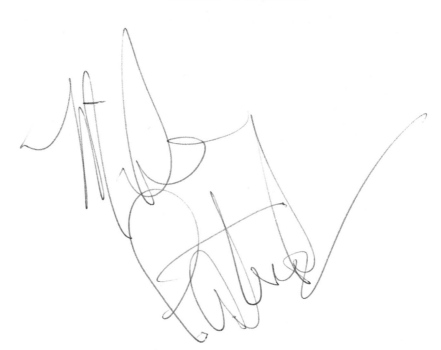

edited by Debby Newman

Published by eBookIt.com

ISBN-13: 978-1-4566-0914-6

In order to learn more about Mike, watch him speak, follow along with him on his incredible journey, download this book as an ebook, or make a business connection to him, you may learn more about him at these three websites:

www.patcom.com

iamnotdoneyet.blogspot.com

www.linkedin.com/in/mikepatrickspeaks

Table of Contents

Foreword i

Acknowledgements v

Introduction vii

Chapter One 1

*September 3, 1971 – My One and Only
Varsity Football Game*

Chapter Two 11

*Reality with Six Weeks of Hospitalization
and Two Extra Holes in My Head*

Chapter Three 19

How Communities Cope With Tragedy

Chapter Four 31

*My Recovery, Facing Stereotypes and Driving
Forces*

Chapter Five 41

Hospital Experiences and Motivation

Chapter Six 51

*Complementing Western Medicine for My
Own Wellbeing*

Chapter Seven 59

An Obstacle Course Called Life

Chapter Eight 69

Using Assistive Technologies

Chapter Nine..**83**

Helping Others Find Meaning

Chapter Ten **93**

Reaching Persons with Disabilities

Chapter Eleven..**103**

Problem Solving Through Role Playing

Chapter Twelve..**119**

Keys to Overcoming Adversity

Foreword

How does someone turn deep personal adversity into opportunity, even inspiration? I am honored to have been asked to write this introduction by the author, Michael Patrick, whom I consider much more than a personal acquaintance. He is constantly searching for ways to improve the lives not only of those with disabilities, but also all of us. After all, no one is without some incapability, some need for the love and assistance of others. We can devote our lives and attention to our personal needs and desires, but everything we do affects our families, our friends, and everyone we touch.

This writer intends for this book to be primarily for members of the medical profession. As a physician, I need to be reminded constantly that I am not just treating someone's illness, but the whole person. Whatever I do, it affects more than just the anatomy and physiology of the patient in front of me. How will it change the life and the relationships of him or her? Can I teach enough about the problem at hand to enroll the patient into the care plan? How much does he understand? How much can I expect him or his caregivers to accomplish? How can I begin to answer these questions without some personal knowledge of his life, his needs at home, his expectations, even his opinions and motivation?

Compassion and treatment go beyond the few minutes spent with one person before encountering the next. As stated by Hippocrates, whose oath most physicians take upon receiving their M.D. degrees, "Life is short, and the Art long; the occasion fleeting; experience fallacious, and judgment difficult. The physician must not only be prepared to do what is right himself, but also to make the patient, the attendants, and externals cooperate."

We live in hard economic times. The general media and even medical journals and papers are touting the usefulness of group appointments with the doctor and establishment of accountable care organizations in an effort to improve "efficiency" of practice. This may really be a euphemism for cheaper care, because the best way to reduce health care cost is not considered to be eliminating the administrators or bidding competitively for the lowest cost pharmaceuticals, to be politically expedient, but rather to ration the use of more expensive tests and procedures. Current accountability means reaching statistical perfection by making 'guidelines' into regulations and treating each problem without regard to the social and psychological needs of the patient.

Ironically, medical schools, including my own alma mater, are now requiring credits in the humanities. One course currently uses close-up magic in an effort to teach students to engage directly with their patients. Rather than teaching magic, I strongly recommend reading this book, then spending the time to learn the emotional status, physical and social needs of every patient in the context of his or her life and environment. The stories told here are highly exemplary. As the author repeatedly contends, "The problem is not the issue. The issue is how you deal with the problem."

"What he has to say may change your life."

There is a symbolic exercise Mr. Patrick describes in this book. He uses it to gain insight into the people he meets. I will leave it to him to interpret but think about societal predation and useful participation. So, how does someone turn personal adversity into opportunity, then inspiration? By sharing experiences and personalizing them to the psychological and emotional needs of everyone you meet, and most especially, those who are dependent upon you for care and compassion. Read on ...

Elliot Francke, MD

Acknowledgements

First and foremost, I want to thank everyone who has read and commented at my blog, I am Not Done Yet and kept in contact with me over the years. Your faith in my ability to get this published worked! I also want to thank Doctors Elliot Francke, Jason Reed and Mark Fallen, all of Abbott Northwestern Hospital in Minneapolis, Minnesota. A special shout out goes to Dr. Tom McIntosh, formerly of Abbott Northwestern Hospital. I could write a whole book on my relationship with him. He is something special and I miss him immensely since he left in 2009. I do not think I would be alive today if Dr. Tom had not been there through my many traumas these last twenty plus years. In addition, thank you Dr. Jeannine Speier of Sister Kenny Rehabilitation Institute and her former colleague Dr. Marilyn Thompson. I want to extend a special thank you to Bob Decker, R.Ph., L.Ac., my acupuncturist since 2003 and Lori Knutson, RN, DSN, HN-BC, the Executive Director of the Penny George Institute for Health and Healing. Of course, I cannot forget the many doctors and nurses over the years that have helped me to have the best quality of life possible for someone with my multitude of medical issues. I would not be here today without the support of my friends and family, especially my mom Colleen Patrick. I greatly appreciate my editor Debby Newman. She helped me take over 20 years of journals and turn them into this book. Also, my long-time friend, Tom Wallace, took the cover photo. Jim Brandenburg took the pictures immediately after my accident. Mike Ross, another long-time friend and my mom, Colleen Patrick, took the other photographs. Finally, I want to say a very heartfelt thank you to all of you and everyone who helped me with this book!

Introduction

In 1971, I faced a life-changing event, when I became a quadriplegic. Since then, I have tried to plant seeds similar to the seeds Johnny Appleseed planted over two hundred years ago. Only, instead of apple seeds, these are seeds of capability. For instance, I have given over 5,500 motivational presentations to youth and adults who work with young people. I also speak to a wide variety of adult groups and tailor my presentation to each group's goals and objectives.

I needed to figure out what the reason was for breaking my neck. I needed to learn why this happened to me and what I was supposed to do about it. Over twenty years ago, I started to journal about my experiences, and they became the basis for my memoir. Writing this book has been a part of my process of self-discovery while turning a tragedy into triumph.

With it, I hope to help people who experience traumatic, life changing events – along with the people who support them. While a majority of my work has involved K-16 students, I have recognized a need to also reach out and help educate medical professionals. Every action we take is important for the people around us – students and patients included. Comments I received over the decades have influenced my healing from Dr. Hallin, who told me to study everything about my body, to the Dairy Queen girl, whose life I helped to save.

I ask you to recognize the important role your attitude plays on the physical, emotional and mental healing process of patients, who may face life-long disabilities and chronic illness. What we say and do affects everyone. Therefore, we must have a positive attitude toward the issues we may face and need to deal with in life. Maybe a reason I got hurt is so you could have the opportunity to read this book.

Mike Patrick

"What he has to say may change your life."

Chapter One

September 3, 1971 – My One and Only Varsity Football Game

"Your head bounced one time, just one time."

Charlie Blackstead
Community College Instructor

In 1971, I was a junior in high school with a plan for my life. I knew where I was going. I was a good student with sports on the brain all the time. I played football in the fall, played basketball in the winter, ran track in the spring and played baseball all summer. I was my class vice-president, a member of the student council, and I had been named to the National Junior Honor Society in the ninth grade. School was easy for me. I was passionate about sports. My goal was to get a basketball scholarship for college. I had many friends and got along with everyone.

The Vietnam War was raging, but it was on the other side of the world, and I really did not think much about it. It did not have anything to do with me. I had uncles that had served and my mom was constantly writing letters to whichever one was in country at any given time. We had a map of Vietnam hanging in our kitchen and we always checked it to know where they were stationed, but it was not real to me because I was going to college, not the military.

My world mainly revolved around my life in Worthington, a small town in Southwestern Minnesota, and whatever sport was in season. I had just gotten my driver's license that spring and was beginning to experience life with the freedom that comes through using the family car occasionally.

Friday, September 3, 1971, was not a typical day. I did not sleep well the night before, in anticipation of our first game. It was going to be the first time I was going to get to play in a varsity game. To say I was nervous would be a huge understatement. Not only was it the first game, but I had a first date that night as well. Becky Geisendorfer was a cute, blonde-haired sophomore who had caught my eye that summer. On the first day of school, I worked up the courage and nervously asked her to go out with me after the game.

I had an odd feeling all that day, which I just chalked up to nerves. I never imagined what was going to happen that night. Nothing was going to happen to me, I was a "hot shot." School and sports were my life. Also, there were college scouts who had come to watch me play that night.

Football was fun. We worked hard that summer. It was supposed to be a "rebuilding year," because we had lost so many of our starters to graduation and not many experienced guys showed up for practice. We all felt good about the coming season, but the local press did not give us a chance to win even half of our games. We only had two weeks of two-a-day practices before school started, so we tried to show up in good shape. We would get a few guys together and play touch football in the evenings, or some of us would get together and run wind sprints and pass patterns. But mostly, we dreamed. I would dream of making a big interception and running it back for the winning touchdown. Nobody had any idea how that first game was going to affect all of our lives so dramatically. All we knew was we had a better team than they were giving us credit for, and we were about to prove it.

We had a pep rally that afternoon. The coaches were introduced to the students, and then our head coach, Mr. Osterberg, introduced the co-captains. They each told the student body how we were going to have this great season and everyone should come to the game that night. The nerves were starting to get a little tense, and by this time, we had the gym full of students really getting noisy. Then Coach Osterberg started announcing the roster for the 1971 Trojans of Worthington High School. Now my heart was in my throat. He went down the list of seniors and made a humorous comment about each one … and then he got to the juniors. When he got to my name, he said, "Mike Patrick, five feet-nine inches tall and one hundred fifty-five pounds soaking wet." I was so excited, as I went down the bleachers, I was afraid I was going to hit a bleacher step wrong and fall flat on my face. The whole experience was extremely exciting, and got everyone ready to go out there and run all over those guys from Owatonna.

Everybody finally left for the day, and we were still excited. This was going be the very first varsity game for many of us, and you could have cut the tension with a knife. I rode my bike home and went down to my room to relax before mom made my pre-game meal of a steak and a baked potato. I tried to rest on my bed, and I listened to my stereo, but there was no way I was going to relax. It was so thrilling thinking about what was about to happen. I would close my eyes and imagine running the opening kick-off back for a touchdown. In each of our kick-offs, I made the tackle. However, those things were not going to happen, since I was not even on the special teams. Still, I went through all of our plays in my head. Everything was just perfect. I had us winning about 42-0. Mom finally called and said it was time to eat. I was so nervous I hardly touched my food.

It was about then I remember a strange, empty feeling starting to develop. It was different, a feeling I had only experienced one time before in a different situation. In the first situation the feeling which some call intuition caused me to change course.

However, this time I did not listen to my intuition. In the past seasons, before a game or a track meet, I would get nervous, but not like this. I did not say anything. I was sure it would go away. I kept telling myself I was just nervous because it was my first varsity game. To this day, I cannot explain that hollow feeling. I was almost nauseous. I could do nothing at home, and I left early for the game. Since it was early, I went for a drive in my dad's pickup around the lake before going to our school. The entire ride was like a dream. That empty feeling would not go away, even as the excitement was starting to build. When I arrived at the locker room, there was only one other guy there. He was Ben Horak, one of our co-captains. Ben was just as nervous as me.

As other people finally started showing up to be taped and get dressed, the adrenalin started to flow. It was getting really noisy as my teammates started to fill the room. All I could think about was getting out onto the field. I could not sit still. I chewed a couple of nails, one so far down it started to bleed. I looked at the first two fingers on my left hand and was proud they had no prints and the nails were rubbed down (I had been spinning a basketball on them for years). That is something I will always remember about that night.

Once I was all dressed, I put my helmet on the floor and used it as a pillow. While trying to relax, I still had that feeling, something was not quite right, but I could not figure out what it was.

Finally, the time came and the coaches came into the room where we were all making last minute preparations. Taping a thigh pad tight, knotting a shoelace, adjusting a chinstrap, tightening shoulder pads or making sure a jersey was tucked in straight. We were all trying to relax. Some of us were lying down on that cold concrete floor. Others were sitting on benches and chairs that were scattered throughout the room.

I remember Coach Osterberg stepping over bodies as he headed for the chalkboard to go over final instructions before we went out to warm up. He went over the special teams assignments, and individually we all thought about our roles. He went over the offense. He discussed several defenses and explained the appropriate times to use each one.

There was so much nervous energy in the room, but as we ran out onto the field, I still had that peculiar feeling. There is no way to describe it; it just did not sit right. I remember seeing the cheerleaders, the fans in the stands and thinking about my first date that night, and I knew she was looking right at me. When I look back on the events of that night, it is almost like a Disney movie, until about half way into the second quarter, when the movie turned into a nightmare.

Owatonna was driving, and they were on our six-yard line. Our starting free safety, Jeff Sellberg, who was one of my best friends, sprained his ankle. As I saw him limping on the other side of the field, I attached my chinstrap — before Coach Osterberg could turn around and summon me into the game. This was IT! I was going into my first varsity game, and I was pumped!

As the free safety, I lined up right over their center and their quarterback. On the second play, I was positioned between our left guard and inside linebacker as the play developed. Their center snapped the ball and double-teamed our guard, and the quarterback handed the ball to the fullback, in the I Formation. As we came closer, I got down, to tackle him low. I tried to get my left shoulder pad about at his knees. My shoulder pads never made it to his knees, because his kneepad caught in my facemask. That action pushed my head down, and drove my chin into my chest. As their fullback lunged for the end zone, I got shoved backwards and ended up on my back, right inside the goal line. I did not know it at the time, but I had just broken my neck.

"What he has to say may change your life."

As the Owatonna fullback lie on top of me, I realized something had gone wrong. My neck hurt terribly, and I tried to move but could not. My arms and legs would not move! I was terrified, in excruciating pain, and I remember this tingling sensation moving down my entire body, right to my toes. Once everyone got off the pile, one of my teammates reached over to pick me up, and I told him to leave me alone. Still, I could not move, and I was screaming in pain. One assistant coach was out there in a flash and crouched over me to see what was wrong. Luckily, there was a doctor at the game, and he came onto the field right away.

Before Dr. Hallin got onto the field, my coach took my helmet off. We should not have done that. I think we panicked and mistakenly took it off. I was probably begging him to remove the helmet. I just do not remember. Once he removed my helmet, Coach Kuiper slowly let my head down to rest on the ground. There was considerable movement in the whole process. I have to tell myself it did not have much of an effect on my paralysis. I truly believe it did not affect my level of function much, if at all.

When Dr. Hallin came onto the field, he took charge. He knew exactly what he was doing. He was very careful in getting a stretcher under me and bracing me, so I could not move.

I remember the pain as if it was yesterday. The back of my neck just pounded, and my head felt like it wanted to blow right off. The throbbing was intense, and there was this very sharp tingling sensation over my whole body. It felt as if thousands of sharp needles were poking me all at once.

I remember I started to cry, because the pain was so intense. It hurt so badly, and there was nothing I could do to stop it. Nobody could do anything to stop it. The looks on everyone's faces were so scary. Everyone looked so serious, and I remember people saying everything was going to be all right. I must have heard that a hundred times those first few minutes.

"You are going to be just fine." "Don't worry, everything will be okay." They wanted to believe that, but like me, they had no idea it was the end of my first life.

Others have told me how quiet everybody in the stands were during those first few minutes while Dr. Hallin directed what was going on, and we waited for the ambulance to get there. Later, in a comment on my blog, one of the students, Carol Radke, not only spoke of the silence; she added that it was a very eerie feeling.

Charlie Blackstead, a math instructor at the community college with my dad at the time of my accident, along with two other instructors from the college, ran the game's chains. Charlie ran the down marker for the game that night. He was right on the line of scrimmage, and he vividly remembers seeing me bounce one time, as I fell back into the end zone at the end of the play.

"Your head bounced one time, just one time," he told me more than thirty years later after he heard me speak. He said, "I can still see it as if it happened yesterday."

When they finally got me on a stretcher and carried me off the field to wait for the ambulance, everyone started to applaud. That has always bothered me to think I had just broken my neck and people were clapping about it. I know they were being polite and they meant well, but I have always felt as if I were a Christian being carried out of the Coliseum.

"What do I do now?" a friend later told me was my date's response to her friend Melissa.

The ambulance attendants were carrying me off the field. Becky and I were supposed to go out to Michaels Restaurant. Michaels was where everyone went after home games. Inevitably, Becky just decided to go home after the game, since I had stood her up and left before the game was even over. The irony of that experience is I was thinking the same thing. I remember thinking during the ambulance ride to Sioux Falls, "What will Becky do now? How will she get to Michael's?" Little did I know what would happen later that night and how my life would be changed forever because of an instant in time.

As they put me into the ambulance, I could feel a blast of warm air from the heater. It was very comforting to get in there and to be surrounded by all of that equipment. My dad came in with me for the ride to the hospital. He kept me from going into shock those first few minutes by talking to me and keeping me calm. He knew what was going on; yet he did not let me know he was very concerned about me. Dad stayed calm that whole time.

The lights started flashing and the sirens were blaring as we went through the streets of Worthington, Minnesota, on our way to Worthington Regional Hospital.

Chapter Two

Reality with Six Weeks of Hospitalization and Two Extra Holes in My Head

"You were my next door neighbor and every morning I would hear you outside shooting baskets while you waited for the bus. You always woke me up with that bouncing. You don't know how many times since that accident I have wished I could hear that basketball bounce outside my window."

Lois Hvistendahl

I remember being in tremendous pain as they wheeled me into that emergency room. I had this uncomfortable brace on my neck to help support it until it was time to take x-rays. My neck was very sore by then. The medical staff took a scissors and cut off my jersey and the strings to my shoulder pads. They really hacked that jersey up before they managed to get it off. The shoulder pads were in pieces when the nurse took them away. They were trying not to move my neck any more than necessary. Next, they cut right up the middle of my t-shirt and tore it off. I was very hot the whole time. The lights were really bright, and my entire neck and head felt like they could just explode.

They took me in and x-rayed my neck, just to make sure of what damage had been done. Until then, I felt as though I was in a dream. Now they had begun to move me around quite a bit, and I could not respond at all.

I was now a quadriplegic, although I did not know it at the time. Nor did I know quadriplegic is the word that describes someone who has paralysis in all four limbs. That is what they call you when you break your neck and damage your spinal cord. I still hate that word, quadriplegic, so usually I just abbreviate it with the word "quad." Quadriplegic has always sounded so cold and harsh.

A feeling of helplessness started to set in as they took me back into the emergency room. Dr. Hallin was considering two choices about where they should take me to see a neurosurgeon, someone who could put me into traction that night. He thought about taking me to Saint Mary's Hospital in Rochester, but that would have been about a four-hour trip. He decided to send me to Sioux Valley Hospital in Sioux Falls, South Dakota, because we could be there in about an hour, and he felt the neurosurgeon there was as good as anybody in Rochester. I have always been thankful he made that choice.

By the time they had me back in the ambulance, Dr. Hallin had put my head in some sort of traction unit. The unit included a strap on my chin to stabilize my neck until they could put me in a more long-term traction unit. When they finally removed the first unit, my jaws were very stiff and sore.

Once we arrived in Sioux Valley's emergency room, a man came up and shaved a strip across the top of my head, while two nurses held me still. I had a hard time keeping my eyes open because of the bright lights and the pain. I just wanted to curl up and go to sleep so it would not hurt any more. Then I heard a nurse say something about morphine.

"They are going to turn me into a junkie right away," I remember thinking.

Someone punctured three holes into my scalp, dabbed them with morphine and then drilled two holes into my skull to insert the Crutchfield tongs that would stabilize my neck, so my cervical spine could heal.

I started to get sleepy, and I must have dozed off, because I do not remember much after that. I do remember people trying to get me into a ward though. My Stryker frame was too wide to get through the door, so they took me across the hall into a private room. That was the last time I was outside of Room 221 for the next six weeks.

Stryker frames preceded halos for stabilizing the cervical spine. A Stryker frame is kind of a sandwich bed. They put me on one so they could turn me from my stomach to my back easily. The Stryker was attached to the bed at each end. It had a top frame and a bottom frame. When the Stryker was hooked up, they could actually flip me from my back to my stomach and to my back again. They did this more than five hundred times over those six weeks!

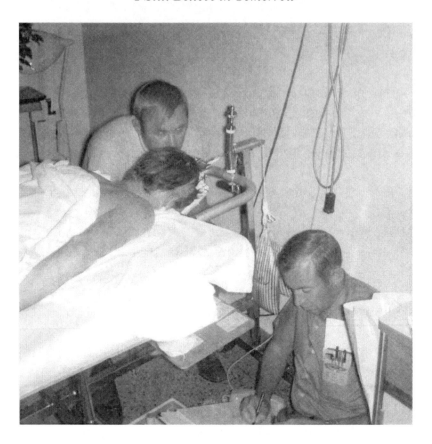

I had to look at the ceiling and look at the floor, over and over again. Here is the nurse getting me strapped in to prepare me to turn me on my back:

"What he has to say may change your life."

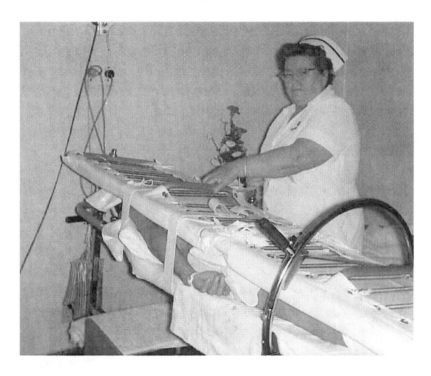

It was not a restful month and a half. I woke up almost every time they turned me, so I rarely got more than two hours of sleep at a time. Once, I slept through two turns in a row and got close to six hours of sleep. Turns are not like flipping over in your sleep. When a nurse prepared me to flip from my stomach to my back, she strapped down the back section first. Then she would grab that black handle on the circle around my knees and pull me to lie on my back for two hours.

My parents were there when I woke up on Saturday morning. We talked about the game. "What was the final score?" I asked. We lost the game. Mom had left the game with Coach Kuiper and came to Sioux Falls. Mom said there was no more scoring the first half after my accident. The next day, my mom read an article from the local newspaper to me. There was a small paragraph about my accident. I remember it was a genuinely uplifting statement about me. Very positive, the kind of stuff you would expect from a local sports reporter. At that time, nobody knew just how bad things really were. Everyone who came to visit was certain I would be all right.

"Just take it easy."

"Enjoy your extended summer vacation."

"You will be out of here in no time."

I wanted to believe them, but deep down inside, somehow I knew I was in for a lot more than I ever could imagine. Those first few days were extremely rough on all of us, and it was only the beginning.

That first Sunday as I laid on my back, my dad raised my right arm straight up in the air. I could see an arm that looked like my arm, but it could not be mine, because my arm was lying across my chest. Or so it seemed. I remember being scared to death, because I could not feel my arm.

During that first weekend, I had conditioned myself to believe everything was going to be just fine. I told myself I was going to walk out of that hospital; this was not going to keep me down. I had convinced myself I was wiggling my toes, moving my fingers and feeling the pinprick tests. I was willing to deal with this on a temporary basis. It was going to take me a few weeks to get back in the action, but only a few weeks. Nobody ever came to me and told me I would never walk again, not until about two months after my accident.

Another life-changing event occurred on the night of my accident, when they inserted an indwelling catheter. From that night onward, having a catheter has affected my quality of life. About six weeks later, they surgically inserted something called a supra-pubic catheter directly to my bladder. The supra-pubic catheter lasted until the summer of 1980.

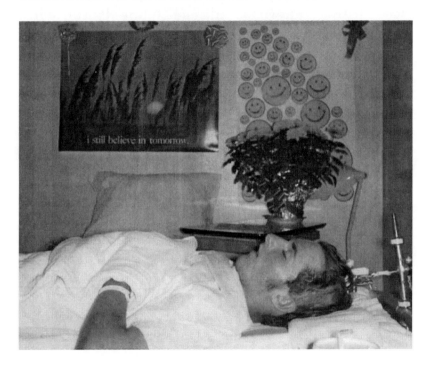

I spent ninety-nine days in that first hospital. Most days were almost party-like, even though there were gauze pads around the holes in my skull, and I could not move.

I kept a registry, which I asked people to sign. It had over twenty-two hundred names in it. People sent me things from all over the country. I received gifts from sports teams and individuals, politicians, recording stars, actors, and most of all, just plain people. It seemed like everybody had heard about my accident, and they wanted to send me their regards. They also sent money, lots of it.

I was the youngest patient on the whole station, and it did not take me long to make a ton of friends. I even made up nicknames for many of the nurses.

One Saturday afternoon, all one hundred twenty-five members of our marching band were on their way home from a parade. Since they were in the neighborhood, they stopped by to see me. Kim Peck, one of the students, recalled years later how only five people at a time were allowed to come in to see me, because there just was not room in my hospital room for more than a few people. She remembers she had to lie down on the floor to look at me, because I was lying in the Stryker frame, facedown at the time she was in the room. Now all these years later, Kim is the director of Rehabilitative Services for the State of Minnesota.

Chapter Three

How Communities Cope With Tragedy

"I think the reason I met you and the special gift you gave me that day was I met you because you are supposed to help me deal with my cancer!"

Jody

There are thousands of resources to help youth deal with community tragedy – currently. When my editor and I did Internet searches with the words, "coping with community tragedy," on a popular search engine, we found over thirty three million references. When we searched the words "high school sports and injuries," we found over one hundred million references. However, in 1971, the Internet did not exist.

In Worthington, Minnesota, the community had to rely on ordinary people to help the youth cope with the after effects of a tragic, Friday night football game. Parents, teachers, school leaders, older siblings and medical professionals helped the young people cope. They needed to help classmates, teammates and others understand how something like this, a popular student's life threatening injury, could happen in "our" community and at a school event. The adults encouraged questions and listened. They helped youth find ways to do their part, such as visiting my room and making cards for me. The point is when tragedy strikes a community; even those people not directly involved in the event may face life-long effects, positive and negative.

Believe it or not, I am still in contact with many Worthington alumni who were touched some way or another by my injury. The best way for us to stay connected is through my Blog, on Facebook and by email. In this post titled, "I Still Believe In Tomorrow," I shared my feelings and asked the readers to share theirs. This post was written September 3, 2009, the thirty-eighth anniversary of a day which is always melancholy for me.

"I decided to write about my feelings in hope it will be a therapeutic session to share them. Forgive me if I don't lie on the couch, because then I could not type," I wrote. The blog included the poster pictured in the last chapter, which a friend gave to me shortly after the accident.

"The quote, 'I still believe in tomorrow' became my slogan, my mantra, and one of my goals," I added in the post. "It was part of the lyrics to a song, 'I still believe in tomorrow, though my life means nothing today,' I continued."

Then I posted, "I felt that way many days, and especially in the middle of countless nights when I could not sleep. There were those feelings of, Why me? When will I wake up from this bad dream? What is going to happen next? What did I do to deserve this? I had many, many questions, and I still do. It is just today the questions are different. I have found answers to many of my questions; however, others remain unanswered. I am guessing many of you can empathize with those thoughts."

I concluded the post with, "Some of you were at the game, some of you have only known me since I became disabled, some of you only know me from hearing me speak and/or reading this blog, and some of you have never met me. I welcome your comments, especially if you were at the game or knew me in 1971. Please let me know your memories and thoughts. Who knows, it may end up in the book. After all, that is the purpose of this whole blog. There, I feel better. Thanks for reading."

Later,

Mike.

I reposted the blog more recently. Between the two posts, I have received dozens of responses from others who remembered my spinal cord injury. Their responses have common threads, including shock, sadness and anger shortly after the accident; followed by my resilience, good humor and inspiration to others over these many years. Finally, "thank you" has been tossed back and forth like a good football. My friends continue to amaze me, and I feel humbled by their positive comments.

To help readers comprehend the intensity and exponential affects on people from this one tragic moment in time, some of their blog excerpts are included below (to read complete comments, you can always visit the post complete with comments by going to this URL:

http://iamnotdoneyet.blogspot.com/2009/09/i-still-believe-in-tomorrow.html).

As you read their comments, think about very fearful events you have witnessed. If you are from my era, you probably remember what you were doing when President Kennedy was shot. A later generation may remember the shock you felt witnessing the fatal accidents of the Challenger and Columbia Space Shuttles. Especially if you were in school at the time, the fatal Columbine School shootings, or in my home state, the killings at the Red Lake Reservation High School, may have left an indelible impression on you. Finally, September 11, 2001 has forever changed the world. Did any of those events help to shape your life?

If you were a young person at the time of an event, the impact of its tragedy may be greater. Most of the comments posted at the blog are from people who were students at the time of my tragedy. Students who witnessed my accident consistently remember the silence.

> All I remember now is standing at the fence in a crowd that was almost silent, waiting first for you to get up and then seeing you being taken away by ambulance. (Amy)

> I was there that night. I remember running around under the bleachers with friends and not really paying very much attention to the game; that is until the ambulance arrived. The crowd was silent and all focus was on the one end of the football field. I remember saying a prayer for you and I am sure everyone else there did as well. It was a quiet and sad walk home from the game that night. (Don Schield)

> I recall your laying on the field for what seemed like an eternity. (Steve Sloan)

> Being four years younger, I was standing in the bleachers watching as much as a seventh grader can. It got very quiet. We knew it was serious because it took so long. Finding out the severity later left such an empty feeling. (Dalen)

There also was much disbelief:

Couldn't believe it when I heard it. (Anon)

I'll admit it; I initially thought the injury wasn't bad. Being in the stands, it was difficult to really see what the real situation was. (Lew)

I saw the play in which you were injured. As I was trying to hold on to the cymbals, I saw the ambulance you were in leave the field between the gate and the hometown locker room. I remember thinking, "What the hell happened?" (Wynn Kirkeby)

All of the neighborhood was in a state of shock and none of us could believe it really happened. (Lois Hvistendahl)

It was my first experience seeing someone with a neck injury and we all thought that you would heal and be back at least to play basketball, which was your favorite sport. When the reality of the irreversible condition set in, we had to accept the gravity of the injury and the death of your dream. (Bruce Ahlberg)

The next Monday at school, it was like what? No! That doesn't happen to a cool guy, it was like pure shock! (Anon)

In addition to disbelief and shock, sadness and anger emerged before healing could occur:

I'll never forget the mad, tearful run home the next day from downtown Luverne, after I heard the news. (Tom Brakke)

I was at the football game that night. What I remember most is the panic and sadness that was present following your injury. I didn't know you well, but my parents were friends of your parents...and my older sister thought you were handsome! So, because of that connection, I felt the "shock and sadness" too. (Paula T)

I do remember the ride home from that game, never did I see such sadness, and concern from my older brothers, and My Mom and Dad. (Sandra Sloan)

Everyone felt just terrible, sad [and] didn't really know what was going to happen and didn't know what to say but waited to hear some news. (Anon)

Healing for many of my friends and acquaintances started after reality set in. It started during my long convalescence in the hospital. I tell medical professionals about these experiences, in hopes the comments will elicit compassion for the people in the lives of their patients. One blogger vividly stated the most memorable visit for all of us.

My most vivid memory was when the entire marching band visited you at the hospital. The staff allowed several students at a time in the room for just a few minutes. They told us to say something positive or funny. You were face down, so we scooted under the bed on our backs so you could see who was talking. I was very nervous and said that we were saving your homeroom seat. You smiled and said thanks but it might be a while. Our group's time was cut short when the staff came in to flip the bed. You made all of us laugh; including your mom, when you said this process was extremely important and necessary to assure that you get 'well done'. (Anon)

What I remember most, Mike, is visiting you in the hospital and then helping to carry you down

the stairs in your wheelchair once you returned
to WHS. Yes, in those days the high school did
not have an elevator. I think your accident made
us all much more aware of (a) people with
disabilities (a phrase that wasn't even in use in
1971) and (b) the fragility of human life, how
things can change so quickly in a mere moment.
(Steve Potts)

After I heard the news, I don't remember
anything else until I walked into your hospital
room and saw you. (Tom Brakke)

I say healing occurred for me and for hundreds of
people who were in my life at the time of my accident,
even though I never was able to get up and walk
again. Dozens of bloggers shared how my accident or
knowing me and witnessing how I have courageously
coped with spinal cord injury and loss of a dream,
along with my many medical problems, has been an
inspiration for them and others in their lives. This
inspiration might have started with the sense of
humor I had during those early hospital visits. If I
could still laugh, maybe they could also. If I can still
believe in tomorrow, maybe they can too. Inspiration
can be infectious! One person posted his own tragic
memory of a single event and its outcome. I am glad
those of us with scars can share experiences with each
other.

I wasn't there that night...but I remember
vividly hearing about it and thinking how awful
-- and how it was amazing it hadn't happened
before. I'm struck by the similarities between
the seminal moments in our lives. There are
moments that irrevocably change our lives
forever. For me, it was when my Father and

Uncle who were my Grandmother's only two sons drowned on a fishing trip to the Oahu Reservoir at Pierre, South Dakota on Memorial Day weekend. I was 12 years old. Like you, I remember every single detail of that day and can recount them as though it was yesterday. In fact, it was 43 years ago. My life went from being an innocent kid on the cusp of being a teenager -- to a kid whose world had just dropped out from under him. I lost my childhood and I carry the scars of that day with me every single day. I'm broken in many ways. I've gone on to do great, fulfilling things -- and "I'm not done yet" either. (Rick Jauert)

We never know when an instant in time will change the course of our life. You may be the person injured, or someone called upon to help healing occur. You can make a difference, as a friend, teacher, parent, nurse, medical technician or stranger on the street. That happened to me.

Several years ago, I did a program for a group of thirty moms. I spent two hours with them and had a wonderful experience. That evening, when I got home, there was an email from one of them, which read in part, "I feel like I've been given a special gift today … Thank you."

That was just one of the highlights of an incredible note that touched me to my core. In my reply, besides saying "Thank you, a couple of times, I wrote, how much her note meant to me and one of the reasons I do what I do is to try to touch people in a positive way. I want to get them to think, and it obviously worked with her that day.

We emailed several times becoming great friends and I did not really know who she was! She wanted to get the set of *Teen Power* books for her daughters (I wrote chapters in three of the *Teen Power* series), and she wanted to meet me at a fun restaurant in my neighborhood for lunch. She even wanted to pay for lunch! I thought that was great, so we agreed to have her come to my house to get the books and we would walk to lunch.

We had lunch at Figlio's in Calhoun Square. Jody grew up close to Uptown and then lived in the suburbs with her husband and daughters. Her father and mother still lived in the house where she grew up, and she loved to come to Uptown.

I will never forget our first lunch; because she expressed how she was so impressed by the way I had learned to solve many small problems and how I developed a positive attitude to deal with my life since my accident. That was in May 1998. Over the next two and one-half years of our friendship, I was always taken back by how she was amazed with my problem solving skills. It did not matter if it was a big problem like how I had to adjust to getting a pacemaker put into my chest, or something simple like picking up a piece of paper with the roll of masking tape I keep on the door lever of my office. She was just impressed by my coping and creative problem solving skills.

I remember thinking Jody would never to be able to deal with a serious problem she might encounter, because I did not believe she had the skills necessary to handle the big stuff. Oh, was I wrong!

I checked my email one day. There was a note from Jody telling me she had been to see a doctor at the

Mayo Clinic in Rochester, Minnesota, and the news was not good. She said she would tell me all about it when I got back. The day after I got home from vacation, Jody came by to help Jayne, another friend of ours, and me to catch up on office work. We were sitting at my dining room table. Jody was at one end, writing out checks and paying bills. Jayne was on one side of the table opening mail, and I was at the other end, reading the mail.

At one point, Jody proclaimed, "I have news I have to tell both of you." She calmly told us the doctors at the Mayo Clinic had told her she had pancreatic cancer. She said, with a big smile on her face, something about the doctors telling her she probably had six to nine months to live!

"There's a four percent chance I'll live as long as five years, and I'm going to beat this," she said.

"Excuse me!" I said, "Did you just say you're going to die before you're fifty? There must be some kind of mistake." Neither Jayne nor I could believe what we were just hearing. We certainly did not expect her news was going to be this! Of all the cancers, pancreatic cancer is one of the worst. It has one of the highest mortality rates and lowest five-year survival rates. Pretty much everybody dies from "pan can," as Jody called it. Then, she said something I will never forget.

"I think the reason I met you and the special gift you gave me that day was I met you because you are supposed to help me deal with my cancer!"

"Excuse me," I said.

"This is not why I met you. At least, this is not why I wanted it to be the reason I met you!"

I could not believe what I was hearing. I could not believe what was happening! I was thinking this could not be happening to one of the nicest people I know! She is not going to be able to deal with the really BIG stuff! Do you remember when I wrote earlier about how I did not think she could handle something extremely difficult?

Well, I found out over the next sixteen months just how well she had learned to deal with the hard problems. That first day, January 16, 2001, she said she was going to beat it. She only beat it by seven months, but she sure was a trooper through the whole process. And she was giving me all of the credit for her newfound coping ability.

"Mike Patrick is the reason I'm handling this so well," Jody shared with her friends and family.

That was hard for me to accept, and frankly, it still is! I have never received a compliment quite like Jody's, nor met anyone quite like her. She had a spiritual awareness, which I realized from that first day of our friendship.

Our friendship also allowed me to be on the opposite side of a tragic experience. The players and the crowd at the Worthington football game witnessed my accident and had all sorts of feelings and life-long effects from it. I in turn, watched my friend die and learned so much from her grace, optimism and perseverance. How might you react when confronted with human tragedy? How might you help others cope?

Chapter Four

My Recovery, Facing Stereotypes and Driving Forces

"Here it comes! He's getting it! Watch this!" The audience buzz was about Dr. Leon Sullivan, also known as The Lion from Zion and one of the biggest activists of the 1960's Civil Rights Movement. "My BROTHER MARTIN!" Dr. Sullivan shouted, slamming his fist onto the podium, while the rest of us sat, feeling the presence of God.

Native American OIC graduation,
Minneapolis, October 23, 1998

I lost my game, in the weeks and months in the hospital following my injury. That is because some people may believe I was going through the first four stages of Elizabeth Kubler Ross' stages of the grieving process. Her stages are:

Denial
Anger
Bargaining
Depression
Acceptance

However, I never really accepted Kubler Ross' grief stages. I was going to walk again! This was not in my plan. I was a hotshot here. I was my class vice president. I was a member of the student council. I had only gotten my driver's license a few months earlier. A couple girls had crushes on me. I had a date that night. This could not be happening to me. But it was.

"I am going to be fine. I am going to walk out of the hospital in a few weeks," I told others, and myself while denying the situation, at first. When I realized that was not going to happen, I became very angry and severely depressed. I did not like the way I looked or felt. I did not like myself. I did not think I had any future. This was the worst time I could imagine. If I could have killed myself, I think I would have. But I could not even do that, since my body would not move!

Two months after I got hurt, Doctor William Church, my neurologist, was having a hard time saying what he wanted to say. I had questions for him, but I could not ask them. After he left the room, I asked the physical therapist who was also there, what I really wanted to know.

"Was he trying to tell me I would never walk again?"

"Yes," she said. Her voice sounded tired. She looked down at the floor. Then, I got angry and had a good, long cry. But when I was done, I was still paralyzed. I still had many questions, and my doctor was gone. Sue was my physical therapist and tried to help by answering some of my questions. I remember it being a very rough day.

"I remember waiting at the door of your room for your return from physical therapy. The instant I saw your face, I knew you had been told," my mother recalled.

Asking questions is not always easy. At times, they may seem nearly impossible to ask. At times, you may not feel strong enough to hear the answer. But asking questions helps us to understand our lives. Like a domino snake, one question can lead to another and another, until finally clarity and understanding can help give us strength.

Months after my injury, I was back in Worthington lying on my physical therapy mat doing range of motion exercises. A large wing-tipped shoe appeared on the mat beside me. It belonged to Dr. Hallin, the same doctor who helped me at the game.

"Learn everything you can about your injury," he said while pointing his finger directly over my face.

He told me to learn everything I could about my situation. He told me to learn about my muscles, their function (or lack thereof), all of my body systems and their status, following the spinal cord injury. He told me to ask questions of doctors, nurses, therapists, counselors ... everybody. He wanted me to be in control and understand what was happening to me. He explained how I would be in the care of people who do not know my situation, and I would need to teach them how to take care of me. It was the best advice I have ever received.

"Remember," he said. "There are no bad questions."

I actually went a little overboard. Although the injury kept me from graduating from high school, when I recovered enough, I went to college. I got my degree in School and Community Health Education from the University of Minnesota. While my classmates were learning about the human body to be teachers and coaches, I was learning about it to understand my injury better. Like most college students, my learning did not just occur in the classroom. I use things from my college experience everyday in my personal life. Before I moved back to Minneapolis and started school here, I took a little diversion.

I moved to Berkeley, California, the week between Christmas and New Year's in 1973. The first person I met was Ed Roberts. He and another pioneer whose name was Hale Zukas were in the Physically Disabled Student Program (PDSP) van, which picked my father and me up at the Oakland Airport. Little did I know at the time just who it was I was meeting. Ed Roberts was the leader in the independent living and disability rights movement. He co-founded PDSP in the 60's when he was going to school at UC Berkeley. He was also one of the first leaders of the nation's first Center for Independent Living (CIL), which was in Berkeley. He also co-founded the World Institute on Disability. We became fast friends. Since I knew Ed, and am old enough to talk about it, some people consider me one of the pioneers in the Independent Living Movement.

However, I was more concerned with my studies than I was about being active in the civil rights movement for people with disabilities. But, I did take part in one sit-in at the California State Assembly building in 1974. I did not see it as that big of a deal; I do not even remember what it was we were protesting. I just remember it rained all day, and we spent several hours sitting in very crowded corridors.

I took two other quads with me, Bill Blanchard and Tim Daly. Like me, they both lived in the Cowell Hospital Residence Program, which Ed was the first resident. We also took a woman who was blind and had a guide dog. The dog was a beautiful Irish setter who stunk to high heaven all the way home, because it was soaked from all the rain. No one said anything about the odor from the dog, but I believe Jane knew her dog was practically gagging the rest of us.

That day certainly did not feel like we were making history, we just did what felt right. Since then, I have been an activist for civil rights by my actions. I share my stories and lessons I have learned to help people realize the problem is not the issue; the issue is how you deal with the problem. This underscores everything I do professionally and how I live my life on a daily basis.

One of the highest compliments I have ever received has been from people who say they do not even see my wheelchair. I will never forget the first time that happened. I was in the hospital during one of my many hospitalizations over the years. One nurse, Nancy Anderson, told me, "I don't even see the wheelchair, and after talking to you for a while you don't seem disabled to me. I know other people that use wheelchairs and they feel disabled, but you don't."

Since then, I have had many people tell me that very same thing, or something similar. I have often asked why they feel that way.

"It's your attitude, Mike," is the answer they almost always give. There it is again, attitude! It really is all about one's attitude! When I was coaching basketball, my student athletes did not seem to notice my wheelchair. This is the 1977-1978 Golden Valley Lutheran College Royals:

On the other hand, some people see my wheelchair, and they start to talk louder, as if me being in a wheelchair means I am also hard-of-hearing. Others assume I am not bright. During school visits, many students have shared their experiences with me. They have told me about their own disabilities and shared how their disabilities have affected their lives. It can be emotionally draining.

For instance, there are places where one would not expect discrimination, but it is there in subtle ways. I like going to the Minneapolis Public Library. The library has many accessibility features, but the depository drawer is not one of them. One day, I decided to go outside and ask a young man who was waiting for a bus to help me return my CD's. He was just beginning to make a phone call on his cell phone when I approached him.

"Sure, I'll help you," he told me.

"I can't talk right now. Call me back in a few minutes, because I'm helping an older man return some CD's into the library," I heard him say to the person at the other end of his conversation.

Now, I was not quite sure exactly how to take his comment about "an older man," since I had never been referred to using those three words before! On one hand, it shocked me he would refer to me as "an older man." On the other hand, I appreciated the fact he did not refer to me as "a guy in a wheelchair."

I told my mom about my encounter and she had a good laugh.

Our family has long been familiar with stereotypes and discrimination. My awareness started in the early 1960's, on the Standing Rock Indian Reservation in South Dakota, where my dad was a teacher and a coach. One of our babysitters was a Sioux Indian whose name was Willard Male Bear. He ran cross country and track, and he played basketball. Willard was also one of our babysitters. He was very quiet and hardly spoke. He entertained us by drawing pictures. He was an incredible artist.

One winter my dad had pneumonia and had to be hospitalized during basketball season. One Friday afternoon before a basketball game, Willard ran home several miles to get a quarter, so he could buy my dad a get-well card. His family lived in a small house about seven or eight miles out of town.

Willard took the quarter to the local pharmacy, bought a get-well card for my dad and brought it up to the hospital. He got to the front desk, and the nurse on duty would not let him go inside to see my dad. It seems they had a rule about Indians not being allowed into the hospital. That same nurse could go to the high school basketball game that night and watch Willard play; Willard just could not go in to the hospital and give his coach a get-well card.

Here is a picture of my dad's A Squad, complete with me as their five-year-old mascot:

On another occasion, after a heart-breaking loss the night before, my dad walked with me for a block and a half to the post office. As we walked past the police station on Main Street, there was a life-sized, stuffed scarecrow body hanging from a rope around its neck. It was supposed to be an effigy of my father. As I understand it, according to the opinion of the people who hung it, my dad played his Indian ballplayers too much the night before, and that was the reason the team lost the game. I was only seven, but I will never forget what we did. Dad did not say anything; he simply looked straight ahead and walked past the people standing around the effigy. As you might expect, we took a different route home.

My dad's contract was not renewed that spring. Before our lives on the reservation were over, my eyes were opened to some of the consequences of racism, bigotry, intolerance, ignorance and lack of understanding. It was the beginning of my lifelong affinity for people that do not fit the mold, people just like me!

Years later, the Native American Opportunities Industrialization Center (NAOIC) in Minneapolis asked me to speak at their graduation ceremony. After my presentation, Clyde Bellecourt, a very active member of the community, made me a Sioux warrior. It was one of my proudest moments. As I left the stage, someone helped the old man who was seated next to me up the ramp.

"Let's see if I've still got it," he said to me.

Dr. Leon Sullivan, a friend of Dr. Martin Luther King, Jr. and the founder of OIC was about to speak. What happened next is something I will never forget! Listening to this legendary person talk about universal human rights left life-changing marks on me as a person and a speaker. At this event where we both spoke, I realized God was working through this elderly man who just a minute ago was struggling to stand up! He was preaching to us from the very depth of his soul, and the audience was right there with him. I do not remember everything he said, but I remember when he slammed his fist on the podium, and forcefully said, "my Brother Martin." It was an amazing seven or eight minutes; and then just like "it" came to him, "it" left him. He was back to being the struggling old man, suffering from the effects of a severe stroke. When the standing ovation was over, he got back to our table and fell that last foot or so onto his chair.

"There, that's how it's done kid," he said as he flashed me a big grin.

"You've still got it Sir!" I replied.

"I just can't keep it very long anymore," Dr. Sullivan quietly said to me and smiled.

Dr. Sullivan was on his game, and I realized then I was in the presence of greatness. Some people, like Dr. Sullivan, have faced discrimination both because of the color of their skin and their disability. Dr. Sullivan was not beaten by either one. For example, he built the sixty-member Zion Baptist Church in Philadelphia; grow into a congregation of six thousand members. He also founded the Opportunities Industrialization Centers to help people find jobs. He marched with Dr. Martin Luther King, Jr. Finally; Dr. Sullivan initiated a code of conduct titled, "Global Sullivan Principles of Social Responsibility." I recommend readers of this book; also discover his code of conduct. It is life changing.

It is partly because of people like Dr. Sullivan I have realized my purpose for being. I know why I got hurt. I do not always like it, but I know the purpose of my accident.

Chapter Five

Hospital Experiences and Motivation

"Holy mackerel!!! That surgeon needs a woodworking course - I could have done that with some dovetail joints and a little Elmer's glue!!"

Roger Knudson
Minnesota Department of Corrections Administrator
February 2006

Giving motivational presentations to young people helps my attitude and motivates me to heal faster when I have to be hospitalized. I have been hospitalized more times than I can count. Several friends simply call Abbott Northwestern Hospital if they have not heard from me for a while. They just assume I have taken up residency there again. I live with spinal cord injury and chronic illness. Together, they necessitate round the clock assistance and frequent clinic visits and hospitalizations. Look at this timeline and imagine how you would plan your life around a "hospital" schedule. Perhaps you will, but as a medical professional rather than a patient.

The longer I live, the more I encounter varied complications; thus bringing new members to the medical team. The team is constantly evolving. If a medical professional did not bother to look at my history and talk to other team members, but simply read a short summary stating, "complicated medical history," on my file, I may not be alive today. It is critical for professionals to understand all of the variables that enter into every patient's experience.

Through all of the hospitalizations and episodes of being home bound for months at a time, I have been able to keep in touch with friends through technology. For example, I sent the following email to explain several months of no contact with most of them.

Subject: Where's Mike Been? Or How I Spent My Summer Vacation
Date: Friday, September 04, 1998 6:10 PM

Hello Everyone!

July 30th to August 25th (Forty-three days),
More than fifty-six thousand dollars,
Scores of Bonanza episodes (three times a night on Fox at 1:00, 3:00 and 4:00 a.m.)
Three squares of hospital gruel every day and
Two surgeries later ...
I now have a new butt and
A new scar down to my knee
That's why you haven't heard from me lately!

In June, I developed another decubitis ulcer on my left ischial tuberosity, just like the one I had back in 1972. As Yogi Berra would say, "Déjà Vu all over again!"

I was on a special bed called a Clinitron. A Clinitron is a twenty-three hundred pound bed of special hospital-grade silicon pellets. The pellets are in constant motion with air blowing up through them. When you are lying on the bed, you are actually suspended on a very thin layer of air. When they turn the bed off for any one of a number of reasons, the air goes out, and you instantly take on the shape of the pellets. It feels like you are lying on the beach.

Best of all, I got my "Summer from Hell!" over with

and only needed one hundred eighty staples to sew up my latest scar! You get good drugs in the hospital folks! You wouldn't believe how many times I heard the statement. "Gee Mike, your butt looks great!"

Later,

Mike

With decades of living with a spinal cord injury, it helps to have a sense of humor at times. In 2003, instead of a traditional Christmas letter, my friends got a hospital chronicle from me. That is because I endured three hospitalizations and one hundred thirty-one days of eating hospital food that year. The bad news is I did not lose any weight, even with having a toe amputated. The good news is I got the hole in my heart repaired and met a nurse who I thought was my soul mate for a while.

Subject: My Latest Story
Date: December 24, 2003 11:09:15 PM CST

Hello One and All:

Some of you have been wondering why you haven't been receiving any emails from me lately so, I want to take this opportunity and fill you in on this loving little saga I like to refer to as "Life" or "Living With Spinal Cord Injury for Thirty-two Years and Counting."

Let's see, I guess I'll start with my life since March twenty-third, when I got to spend twelve days in Abbott Northwestern Hospital, here in lovely South Minneapolis in a nice, quiet neighborhood affectionately known by many as "Crack Alley." I am not saying it is a bad neighborhood or anything, but the neighborhood parks and recreational center had a bright neon sign out front that read "Sunny's Bar and Grill." You could almost always "score" some sort of illicit drug from one of the ever-present "coaches" who recruited out front. Judging by the clothes they wore and the nice cars always parked in front of this recreation center, they were very successful.

Moving right along to July seventh, which for those of you who do not know, was two days after my thirty-year class reunion in Worthington. That was funny, because I never graduated from high school. Back to July seventh, when I was sitting in a clinic located on the beautiful Abbott Northwestern campus and receiving an IV infusion of a somewhat powerful antibiotic whose generic label is "Somewhat Powerful Antibiotic." The drug is also referred to in the medical field as Vancomycin, when something miraculous happened.

After the experience, I began to understand what an epiphany must be like. Let me describe the "episode." I noticed a sensation moving up my right leg, which I can only describe as a ring of energy that felt like a ring of electricity or tiny lightning bolts. The sensation was interesting, because it was exactly like the feeling I had when I broke my neck, only it was going in the opposite direction. As it moved up my leg, I remember thinking, "This can't be happening. I'm paralyzed!"

The sensation continued up my right side, down my arm and up the right side of my face. The right side of my lip and tongue went numb, feeling as if I had just gotten a shot of Novocain. My sight got blurry, my voice slurred and I got somewhat confused. They asked several questions I could not answer, like not knowing it was Monday. I did know who the president was though. I told him, "You mean the a**hole?" Remember, I did say, "somewhat confused." I had not lost it all!

It was very scary, and I started to pray this was not the end of my life, as I know it. Needless to say, I was very relieved when the sensations started to recede and my faculties started to come back. I had two or three more of these "episodes," and the medical professionals are still not sure exactly if they were strokes, seizures or pulmonary emboli (blood clots in my lungs). I'm pretty much back to my pre-Vancomycin status. I can't say "normal" because I have never been "normal"!

So where are we? March in and April out; July in and August out; August twenty-eighth to December first; back to my home away from home in Room 3152. From August first to November twenty-seventh, I left my bed/beach home twice — once for surgery and once for a CT scan. Later, Mike

In 2005, the hospitalization I most remember happened after I broke my ankle. December twentieth, a fill-in personal attendant dropped me while trying to transfer me into bed. Three firefighters came and got me back into my bed. I sweated all night, but just on the right side of my head, so that meant something was wrong on my left side. This phenomenon of symptoms occurring on the opposite side of one's body is called autonomic dysreflexia (AD) or hyperreflexia.

The morning personal attendant arrived to find my left ankle swollen and blue. When he lifted my leg, the ankle just dangled. We went to the ER, and x-rays confirmed both the tibia and fibula were cracked. On

Christmas Day, surgeons inserted nineteen screws and two metal plates into my ankle. I was allowed to leave after fifteen days in the hospital. When the doctor told me I would be using a walking cast, I had to chuckle a bit.

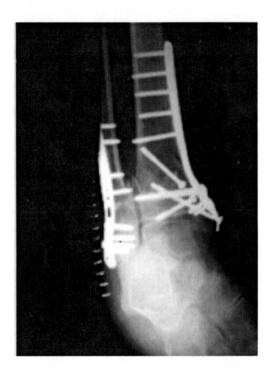

"At least my cast is walking," I thought to myself. Friends told me the metal in my ankle meant I was going to have a hard time getting through airport security. However, they had not thought about the 300-pound power wheelchair I already had been maneuvering through the gates.

Earlier, I mentioned the need for a sense of humor. For instance, the walking cast is a bit of dark humor. I will share a few other reactions I got following the Christmas surgery.

"Stay away from magnets," said Earl.

'Sir, this rope's a little tight,' is what we in prison say," shared Roger, the same person who commented about Elmer's glue and this surgery, at the beginning of the chapter.

I was fine for a while after that, but in August of 2006, something was going on in my body that was producing incredibly violent spasms that were very much out of control. One day, because of the violent spasms, it took six people to get me into my wheelchair. They tried several drugs to quell the spasms. The spasms did not go away until they gave me a muscle relaxer called Marinol. Marinol's active ingredient is THC, the same active ingredient found in marijuana.

Like former President Clinton, I did not inhale! They gave me a five-milligram dose a few times. After seeing the reaction to that dosage, Dr. McIntosh reduced it to a two point five milligram dose. He did not keep me on that dosage very long either since the spasms were starting to decline.

When I was growing up, my father was a coach, and there was never alcohol, drugs or tobacco in our house. Once I started playing organized sports in the seventh grade, it would have been breaking training rules to use any illicit substances. Besides, they were illegal for a young teenager! I never wanted to risk not being able to compete and so the big three were never an issue in my mind.

Besides breaking training, I would have been letting down not only my father but my mother as well. That was something I was never going to do.

I find it very ironic, that my first experience with THC came shortly after my father's death on July 23, 2006. I have often wondered what he would have done, or how he would have reacted had he seen me giggling incessantly while I was high on Marinol. Part of me wants to know how he would have reacted, but the other part is glad he never saw his son high on drugs, even though my doctor prescribed them.

I must say while I was under the effect of the Marinol, friends and family who came to visit thought it was very funny watching me entertain them by doing nothing but giggling! I never got the munchies. I just laid there and giggled! I also had what I thought were profound insights. Like, I wondered why they call what doctors do "practice." I hoped they would one day get it right and not have to practice anymore.

Seriously, I have been working with several excellent doctors at Abbott Northwestern Hospital and Sister Kenny Rehabilitation Institute in Minneapolis for many years now. All of them are excellent in their specialties, and they bend over backwards to give me quality care. I am on a first-name basis with most of them. Because I spend so much time in their clinics and as an in-patient, I have developed a very special relationship with quality people. One of my doctors looks so young I like to call him "Doogie," referring to Neil Patrick Harris, who played the role of a genius teenage doctor in a television sitcom titled, "Doogie Howser, M.D. One day, I was being transported from one station to another by three staff members and ran into Doogie in the hallway.

"Doogie, where have you been?" I said. We spoke for a while and headed off in different directions. One of the nurses asked me, "You don't call Dr. Reed 'Doogie,' do you?"

"Sure," I said, "doesn't everybody?"

They were mortified! Of course, they do not call him "Doogie." They have a professional relationship with him, and out of respect, they call him Dr. Reed. They could not believe I had the irreverence to call him by that nickname. He and I have a great relationship, which is why we can laugh at a simple nickname.

At the beginning of this chapter I said, "When living with spinal cord injury it helps to have a sense of humor." I believe that likewise for medical personnel who work with us on a daily basis.

Chapter Six

Complementing Western Medicine for My Own Wellbeing

"Change is the inevitable factor on which all life depends. Through all change, comes good and bad, do not dwell in the bad for it will consume you. Instead, focus on the good and learn from the bad to create a greater change in you and those around you. Do not fear it or attempt to alter it either, for it is folly. Take change as it comes and be thankful for it. For this is the constant unpredictable pattern of life."

Nick, 8th Grade,
March 6, 2003

I received the above wonderful statement from a young man in an email. I believe he says it all. Since my accident in 1971, if you add up all of the time I have spent in hospitals, it is somewhere in the vicinity of four years. At the same time, change is always present for me. I have always felt like I have had two lives. The one before my accident lasted a little more than sixteen years. The one after my accident has been growing since that night.

Christopher Reeve, who played Clark Kent/Superman, only lived nine years after his horse riding accident when he broke his neck. My doctors keep telling me it is guys like me who are breaking new ground for living long lives after suffering a spinal cord injury. With advances in medical science, they keep finding ways to address all of the issues that can threaten my mere existence and the other 265,000 spinal cord injury survivors in the United States! Reeve's adult children have stayed committed to survivors with a foundation established in their father's name.

Another resource for spinal cord injury, the National Spinal Cord Injury Database, was founded in 1973. It has followed some spinal cord injury patients for over thirty-five years after their injury. During that time, the causes of death, which appear to have the greatest impact on reduced life expectancy for us are: pneumonia, septicemia and pulmonary emboli (taken from: https://www.nscisc.uab.edu). In 2009, the NSCI reported 14,390 spinal cord injuries, of which less than 8% were sports related. However, the American Association of Neurological Surgeons reports football as being related to 300,000 concussions annually (taken from: http://www.aans.org). Sports participation contributes to healthy lifestyles, but I am happy more safety precautions are in effect now than in 1971!

I have had so many medical problems; I cannot begin to list them all here. From the very beginning, I have had problems with all of my major body systems starting with my urinary tract, which has been a severe issue, my entire post injury life. I am now down to one kidney and doctors have had to reroute my urinary tract on several different occasions.

Surgeries

Remember the night of my accident? I had an indwelling catheter inserted, which lasted six weeks. Shortly after I got out of traction, doctors inserted a supra pubic catheter, which lasted until 1980. Then in 1980, the catheter was replaced with an ileal loop. The 1980 surgery was a "butcher job," which had to be redone again, four years later. Why? The doctor made a fifteen-inch ileal loop, which has caused me to have a constant urinary tract infection ever since. When he placed the first ileal loop, he took my bladder out and ran both of my ureters into the loop. He told me this surgery would need to be re-done every few years.

I found out from Dr. Fallen, my current urologist, once the surgery is completed, there should be no need to redo it, ever! For instance, I have two friends who have had ileal loops since 1963, and they rarely have any problems with them. Dr. Fallen has had to take out my left kidney and continually find ways to try to stave off urinary tract infections and other problems that were results of the original, extra long illeal loop. Dr. Fallen just exudes confidence. He is one of those surgeons who can be trusted implicitly with everything he does.

He could remove the extra long loop to eliminate the problem. However, as previously stated, he believes I might not make it off the table, because the surgery would be very complicated due to the scarring around the loop, and it would be an extremely difficult operation. I appreciate his candor, and so, we deal with the problem with many treatments of antibiotics.

One day I overheard Dr. Fallen showing his nurse two x-rays of illeal loops, one he did on another patient and mine. In comparing the two x-rays, he showed her the three- to four-inch conduit he put in his patient. Then, he showed her the fifteen-inch conduit in what he referred to as "Poor Mike's" loop.

I got a charge out of his reference to "Poor Mike's" loop! That is not the only bad surgery report I have received over the years. I have had my share of doctors who did not necessarily fit in the top of their class. I like to tease doctors and ask them if they know what they call the doctor who finishes last in his or her medical school class. When they reply they do not know the answer, I tell them, "They call him or her doctor!"

Complementary Treatments

At times, I have chosen alternative or complementary treatments when traditional medicine has not been effective. For instance, I had been going from one antibiotic to another, and I still had almost constant urinary tract infections.

Vinegar – A Home Remedy

My good friend Owen Orthmann, who is also a quad, told me of an old, home remedy, of which he had just learned. I have started becoming a drinker and drink three cocktails a day. I put a teaspoon of apple cider vinegar and a teaspoon of honey in eight ounces of water. The first time I drank it, I did not get a UTI (Urinary Tract Infection) for five months! I have not had another nice long five-month run of an infection-free urinary tract. However, with this cocktail, I have occasionally gone four to six weeks without needing to take a urine specimen into the lab for analysis. That is better than every ten to fifteen days without infection prior to drinking these cocktails! When I told Dr. Fallen about my discovery, he had already heard of some of the healing qualities of apple cider vinegar.

Acupuncture

Another alternative treatment I have been utilizing since 2003 is acupuncture. Two acupuncture treatments a week have been a tremendous experience for me. They have allowed me to stop using sleeping pills and pain pills, sped up healing times on a couple of occasions, allowed me quick, twenty-minute, Bi PAP-free naps twice a week, decreased several pain issues and have given me a general feeling of calmness.

I have developed a wonderful relationship with a specific acupuncturist, Bob Decker. He is very in touch with Eastern medicine, and we have great conversations while he needles me up so I can "cook" for twenty minutes. He has an amazing demeanor and provides an extremely calming effect on me. The alternative medicine practitioners and office staff at the Penny George Institute for Health and Healing (affiliated with Abbott Northwestern Hospital) tell me I am like a puddle after I come out of one of his treatments.

I use acupuncture to supplement a Bi PAP machine and more traditional sleep treatments for my sleep apnea. I was diagnosed with sleep apnea in 1997. Even with various prescriptions, I often woke up several times a night, and my sleeping patterns were not very good. I have had three or four sleep tests and found out I wake up and go to sleep one hundred twenty times per hour. That is once every thirty seconds, I wake up and go back to sleep, if I am not using a Bi PAP machine to help me breath while I sleep.

Because of the constant waking up and going to sleep, I could never get into Rapid Eye Movement (REM) sleep. Therefore, I would wake up in the morning more tired than when I went to bed. I know I sometimes get into REM sleep now because I dream. My dreams are very vivid and often mirror something that happened during the day. I reach REM sleep when I use the Bi PAP machine. I also reach it during acupuncture treatments.

Hypnosis

Another alternative I use is self-hypnosis. I listen to a CD that puts me into a state of self-hypnosis. The hypnotist is a friend of mine by the name of Jim Wand. I have given talks with him at probably a dozen or more teen leadership programs. He has a Ph.D. in psychology with an emphasis in hypnosis and has a lucrative speaking career. I think Jim Wand a GREAT name for a hypnotist!

His technique has worked for me countless times, despite the fact I have a mild brain injury! In 1984, the temporal occipital lobe of my brain went without oxygen for about six minutes. The temporal occipital lobe governs field of vision and short-term memory.

I went through a seizure like episode and became unconscious. My personal care attendant called 911. Although the paramedics carried equipment into my room, they never gave me oxygen. I still have the oxygen cannula from that experience! When we got to the hospital, the paramedic told the head nurse in the emergency room, "I don't think there's anything wrong with him. I think he's just a heavy sleeper."

When I woke up the next day in the intensive care unit, I looked at a clock and could not see from 6 to 12. I had a partial field cut on the left side of my brain. In the next twenty-four hours, I got the lower left quadrant back and now only have an upper left field cut. However, I still cannot see from nine to twelve on the face of a clock.

In regards to damage to my short-term memory, medical professionals told me if I worked on it, I could probably get much of that back. So, that is one of the things I work on. When I give a speech and ask someone their name, I will often go back to that person and call him or her by their name. I do not always get it, but it is something I work on. People often think it is cool I remember their names. Little do they know I remember and repeat their names to exercise my temporal occipital lobe.

For example, once I did a program for University of Minnesota health career students. I asked the names of all of the twenty-eight participants. Fifteen minutes later, I repeated twenty-five of their names. Within another five minutes, I remembered the twenty-sixth name and five minutes after that I recalled the twenty-seventh name. I believe I was unable to repeat the twenty-eighth person's name, because it was in an East Indian name. I was not familiar with that name. If I went under hypnosis, I probably could still recall the name today.

I have learned a great deal about myself by practicing self-hypnosis. Jim's CD focuses on memory. He emphasizes how we can train our brains to choose to remember instead of choosing to forget. The biggest thing he addresses for me is short-term memory. He discusses how we always make excuses for things like not remembering someone's name. He says it is a learned behavior, and he is absolutely right. He says everything we have ever heard, seen, done or read is in the subconscious brain. The trick is to pull it out and get it into the conscious brain. Getting it into the conscious brain can be done with practice. I continue to practice. My short-term memory ability of name recall is living proof you need to "use it or lose it."

Blending East and West

I am a very strong believer in integrative medicine. I believe as we become more and more of a global society, those who have primarily studied Western medicine will study Eastern medicine and integrate the two disciplines. After all, the Chinese have been successfully practicing acupuncture, healing touch and guided imagery, among other healing techniques for more than six thousand years. Eastern medicine traditionally looks at the whole person, rather than parts of a person.

However, it takes more time to assess and study the whole patient, rather than a symptom. That can be challenging for a practitioner who has limited amounts of time. Because of people I know who have been weaned from excess medicines and unnecessary surgeries, I believe that extra time is well spent.

The Western medical community is starting to accept other types of treatments as being credible and helpful. For instance, some insurance companies cover chiropractic treatments and some cover acupuncture, healing touch and massage, naturopathic and homeopathic modalities, along with exercise and health counseling. One would need to have been living under a rock to be unaware of the important role health, exercise, mental and spiritual practices play toward our health. If we think about the advances that have been made in the way medicine is practiced during the last forty years, just think about the changes we will see in the next forty years!

Chapter Seven

An Obstacle Course Called Life

"...I wish you die and go to hell"
(High School Student) Name withheld
November 2005

With more than fifty-five hundred speeches under my belt, I do not remember all of them. If I focus, chances are good I will remember something that made each day special, not only to me, but also to another person. Responses are almost always expressions of appreciation for helping someone get through a very difficult period in life, for understanding their personal obstacles or for opening their eyes to what people with disabilities experience.

"What he has to say may change your life."

Obviously, the student who sent the email that opens this chapter had anger issues that needed to be addressed. It is even more frightening he included a picture of me from my Website, which he had defaced with red and blue paint, probably by using a software program. Once I alerted his school principal, the student sent an apology, and I forgave him. Here was a person of authority who helped open the door for a student who was facing obstacles to receive the help he needed. I hoped I made a difference in speaking and in my act of forgiveness. Making a difference is one of the reasons why I love what I do for a living.

In Chapter Four, I mentioned there was a reason for my accident; in part, it helped me to confirm my reason for being! I could not imagine getting a real job. You have heard people say, "If you love what you do, you will never work a day in your life." That is the way I feel. I cannot wait until I give my next speech.

I found my passion at an early age. I have my ninth grade speech teacher to thank for that. Little did I know when I first came into her classroom, Miss Doman was to become my all time favorite teacher, life-long friend, mentor and the main reason I became a professional speaker.

On the first day of her class, I was speaking with a nasal twang and all of my classmates were laughing. This young, single and attractive teacher had no idea I was not using my regular voice. When I came in on the second day and spoke in my real voice, she was not amused at my childish prank. However, we boys had found great joy pulling one over on the new teacher. Later she told me she had thought the laughing boys were being cruel to me.

As the school year progressed, that teacher gave me an opportunity, which made me realize how much I love being in front of an audience. She came to me one day and told me I was going to emcee the All School Annual Variety Show. I told her I did not want to be the Emcee.

"I'm not asking," was her rather tort reply.

"You will get up in front of the whole school and tell some silly jokes in between acts. Everyone will laugh at you. You will have a great time and will not want to get off the stage," she said. Recently my mother was going through boxes of my old school papers when she ran across my notes for the Variety Show on April 8, 1970! What a wonderful find. It was my first experience on stage and I loved it! She was correct. I did not want to get off the stage that day.

Now more than forty years later, I still do not want to get off the stage. My speaking is like therapy for me. Speaking about my life experiences has given me an opportunity to make a small difference in many people's lives, just as Miss Doman's teaching made a difference for me. Her teaching affected more students than me. It also affected the entire student body of another school. In an ironic twist of faith, she transferred to the Owatonna schools and taught the person I had tried to tackle during that fateful football game.

In addition to my speaking passion, I keep getting new material to present. I am always facing new obstacles to overcome and then finding new ways to overcome those obstacles. If it were not for all the experiences I have had to deal with I would not be where I am today. I have a speaking job that allows me to share my original injury, resulting complications and what they have meant for the rest of my life. Unfortunately, the speaking engagements sometimes have to wait because of my health obstacles. I see this book as an extension of my speaking passion, allowing me to reach additional audiences, such as medical professionals.

In 2000, I was flying to California to speak. I usually fly with my personal care attendant, but that particular day I flew alone. My younger brother, Chad, was going to help me get off the plane and take care of me for the weekend. Because of my disability, I am always the first one on the plane and the last one off. Like other occasions, the airlines gave me the front row seat of first class, because it was not sold and it was easier to get me in the wider, more accessible seat.

When they started to board the rest of the first class passengers, I recognized the second man. He was an identical twin, who had been a year behind me in high school. He and his brother were minister's kids, good students, who were never in trouble. I looked at him, and at first I was not sure which twin he was. All of a sudden, something came over me and I just blurted out, "Percy Kallevig, how are you?"

Remember, it had been about twenty-eight years since I had last seen him. He replied, "Mike, I didn't recognize you. I watched them helping you get on the plane and I wondered to myself — I wonder what Mike Patrick is doing today?"

I said with a smile, "Getting on an airplane."

Since everybody was boarding now, he got in his seat across the aisle and back one row from me. The man standing right behind Percy sat down next to me and I told him one of those "small world" stories about how Percy was a year behind me in school thirty years ago! When everybody else had boarded the plane, Percy leaned forward to try and tell me something. As he did, the man sitting next to me asked if we would like to sit together. They switched places and the next three and one-half hours literally changed my life. Percy and I swapped stories reminiscing about the time around my accident.

I remember one story he told which I have used in speeches since then. As I said, Percy's father was a minister and they all went to church on Wednesday nights. Percy asked me if I remembered a guy by the name of Rick Van Roekel."

"Sure," I said, "He was one of my best friends. He was also our right defensive end on the play when I broke my neck. He is now the head football coach at the high school in New Ulm, Minnesota. He has been a teacher and coach there for many years."

Percy continued, "After church on Wednesday nights he and I would often go driving around and a couple of times we came out and picked you up and the three of us drove around for a while. I never felt like it was Mike and Rick riding around with Percy, or Mike and Percy riding around with Rick, I always felt like it was Rick and Percy that got to ride around with Mike Patrick."

"Why would you say that? Why did you feel that way?" I asked.

"You were just always one of those special people."

Percy used this really cool analogy about the people on the plane, "There are all those people back in coach class who think we must be something special because we are sitting in first class. We both know why we are really here. You are up here because they couldn't fit you into your seat, so they put you in the front row of first class because it was easy to get you in that seat. I am sitting up here not because the church where I now minister paid for a first class ticket, but because I knew the pilot and they had an empty seat. So I got a free flight."

In high school, you were always first class and we were always just coach. So when you got hurt it affected us all very deeply. I remember where I was the night of your accident. I was at my girlfriend's house and some kids came over after the game. They were all upset and they said Mike Patrick is paralyzed. I'll never forget it, my girlfriend started crying."

I asked him, "Why would she cry? She didn't know me?"

Percy quickly responded, "Everybody knew you. You were friends with everybody. You talked to everybody. I wasn't on the football team, but you still made me feel good about myself. I always knew one day I would get to tell you some of these stories, and now, twenty-nine years after your accident, I am finally getting the chance."

"I didn't think those nights we went driving around were any big deal." I said. That is when I realized they were a big deal to Percy.

You never know how the things you say and do are going to affect people. Your words and your actions might make a huge difference to your friends or to that person you never felt like was a part of your group. Do not let it take thirty years for you to tell someone how he or she has affected your life — perhaps only by doing something as simple as riding around in a car or playing on the same team. It might be something you say in the cafeteria, in a classroom or walking home from school. Leaders make a difference every day whether or not they even think about it.

After that conversation, I told Percy part of our conversation would be part of a speech. Percy, who is now a minister, (as is his twin brother) told me, "Oh Mike, some of this is going to be part of a sermon." I have told this story a number of times since then in schools and conferences around the country. That three and one-half hour plane trip really made me realize how important the things I say and do really are. I always knew that, but my conversation with Percy made me think about it even more.

As I have mentioned, your words, actions and your deeds can make a huge difference to others. The person in front of you may have a medical history of which you are not aware. Like me, they may have multiple health issues and chronic illness. You may be seeing them for something simple like a cold, or for a specific condition, but it is helpful to respect the patient as a whole person, not just by what is in the file in front of you. Better healing will occur if you treat patients as unique individuals and reach out to each one of them as a whole person, not just a medical symptom.

In addition to maintaining a holistic attitude toward each patient, remember you are part of a team. Good medicine truly takes a team approach. Everyone from the nursing assistants, to surgeons, specialists and nurses must bring their "A Game" to each patient, especially patients with complex medical needs. Besides always bringing your "A Game," when making decisions and treating conditions, communication with the other team members is extremely important. While reading the timeline of health challenges I have faced, think of the extra complications someone like me might have faced without good communication between my medical team members.

Sometimes I wonder how it is I am still alive. At one presentation in Iowa, I told the students about my younger sister Kathleen, the only person who remembered what a doctor told my family shortly after my accident. He said my life expectancy following the accident was nine years. That is how long Christopher Reeve, the Superman actor, survived after his horse accident, and he had money for the best medical care in the world.

"Why am I still here?" I rhetorically asked the students at that Iowa presentation.

When I asked that question, a young boy, without flinching or moving a muscle, replied, "Cuz' you're not done yet." That is how I got the title for my blog!

If I had not played football that night in 1971, would I have gotten hurt some other way? Obviously, there is no way to know what my life would have been like had I not gotten hurt, but it sure would have been nice to find out. I do not know what opportunities I would have had if I had not broken my neck. I think about that often and wonder where I would be and what I would be doing if it had not been for that "instant in time."

Perhaps I still would have been a motivational speaker. I might have been like the late Chris Farley, who used to play a character named Matt Foley on *Saturday Night Live*. The guy was a motivational speaker who lived in a van down by the river.

I think we all experience those feelings on occasion and wonder what our lives would be like if only we had made one decision over another. One of the hardest things for me to deal with is the inability to make decisions because of my disability. Yet, when I am confronted with an issue, I often hear myself saying, "Remember Mike, the problem isn't the issue, the issue is how you deal with the problem."

Chapter Eight

Using Assistive Technologies

"Beowulf empowered himself to kill Grendel (and Grendel's mother). He did not give in to fright. Neither did Mikey. Mikey could have given into fright at any time ... He told my mom that when the doctors said he would never do certain things he had to empower himself. I have no doubt that he was frightened for his life. Instead of giving into fear, Mikey rose above it so to save himself. He did not give in to fear and surrender his battle for life."

Jenna Wright, 7th grade
May 2007

The hardest thing for me to do is to ask for help. I do not feel disabled until I have to rely on someone else to accomplish a specific goal. I have always said, "I try to live my life despite my disability, rather than with regards to it."

There are four things that frustrate me because I have no control over them:
1. When my van does not work
2. When my wheelchair does not work
3. When my body does not work
4. When my computer does not work.

Mobility Issues (frustrations number one and two)

I am a professional speaker who travels across the country, by airplane and by driving my van. I offer programs for people of all ages. I always try to leave time for questions and people always have lots of them. Sometimes, I learn about their comments later. For instance, a teacher named Stacy sent this message after a presentation in St Paul.

"One of my students asked if he could tell me his dream. I told him sure. He said that his dream is to trade places with you so that you could have your dream and walk. His name is [also] Mike, and I thought you'd like to know."

My all-time favorite comment happened one day when a fourth grader asked me, "How do you get gas?"

"It usually comes from eating a school lunch." I coyly replied.

"No, no, that's not what I meant," he said after all the students stopped laughing. "What I mean is, how do you get gas in that special van you drive?"

"That's a different question. If you don't ask a specific question, you probably won't get a specific answer," I replied.

My response came out that way because I want students to think about the questions they ask before they ask them. I believe if one thinks about a problem and what they need to know to help with their own situation; chances are pretty good they will ask questions, which help them to find the best answer.

"The problem isn't the issue, the issue is how you deal with the problem," is my motto.

My van is specially equipped with hand controls, so I can drive it. It also has a ramp, so I can get in and out, and it includes voice recognition, blue tooth car phone.

In addition to my van, my motorized wheelchair is a principal mode of transportation for me. When something as simple as a flat tire on my van or my wheelchair happens, I am stuck. There is absolutely nothing I can do about it. I am completely helpless. To top it all off, I usually get a flat tire on my chair on a Friday afternoon at about 4:30! The frustration lies in the fact I cannot do anything about it.

At times, I require help from others, even with assistive devices like the folding ramps I carry in the back of my van. On August 10, 1994, I arrived at Crossroads, a juvenile facility for youth who had made at least one bad decision and gotten caught. I pulled into the parking lot and there were six steps going up into the house. I did not know what I was going to do, so I drove around the building to see if there was an entrance without steps. There was no wheelchair accessible entrance, so I got out of my van just as the director was coming out of the building. He asked me if they could help me get up the steps.

I do not like being carried into a building, but sometimes there is simply no way around it. My ramps are designed for an incline of three or maybe four steps. Six steps are pushing it! They had four young men help me up the steps on my ramps. It was a very steep incline and for a minute, I did not know if we were going to make it to the top. We made it, and I thanked the young men for helping me. I then spent the next ninety minutes or so talking to them about the things I address in most of my presentations. I talked about consequences, perceptions, honesty, relationships, self-esteem and creative problem solving.

Usually I talk about trust too. For some reason that day, I forgot to mention anything about trust. On the way out of the building, and immediately after, as I showed them my modified van, I found out why I did not mention trust, I was supposed to show them.

Four of the boys helped carry my chair and me down these steep steps on the chair's back wheels as we guided it on the ramps. As we were descending, I heard someone tell the director, "He really trusts those guys, doesn't he?"

"Yeah," he said, as he stood there astonished, with his mouth wide open.

Health professionals often have similar opportunities to let their patients take the lead, which can demonstrate their trust in each patient's own knowledge about their illness. By trusting these young men to lead me, they gained confidence. When we got to the bottom, I thanked them and we all went over to look at my van. We were standing by my van as it started to rain, and I asked the teenager closest to the van to open the door.

"You mean it isn't locked?" he said.

On that particular day, I instinctively knew it was not necessary to lock my van. Like-wise, health professionals learn to trust their instincts when practicing good medicine. I guess I needed to walk my walk while I talked my talk to this specific audience.

Many of the places where I speak have ramp entrances, but getting up on stage is a whole other matter. Since passage of the Americans with Disabilities Act, some of these architectural issues have been addressed by Universal Design principles.

However, I have faced a few frightening moments where that was not the case. For example, Tim, my care attendant and I were wandering outside in a parking lot at a hotel where I was supposed to speak. It was a beautiful July Virginia night with very few stars. The parking lot was dark; there were not lights. The sidewalk was very new and since the Americans with Disabilities Act was passed way back on July 26, 1990, I felt very safe in knowing there would be a curb cut at the end of sidewalk. I was wrong!

My head hit pavement with a resounding thud! When I went off the curb and down on to the new, black asphalt, I found out in a hurry the asphalt in Virginia is just as hard as the asphalt in Minnesota. Although the new, white sidewalk appeared to be ramped, it was very dark outside.

Tim was only a few steps away and did not actually see me go down. He said later he just heard the crash and came over to help get my chair off me, and turned me over so I was lying on my back. I told him to go inside and get someone to help get me back into my chair. Before long, there were several people coming to my assistance. I think three or four people put me back into my chair.

I could feel blood running all over my face and on the top of my head. As you may know, scalp wounds bleed profusely. I had several scrapes running from my chin to my forehead! When we got back to our hotel, I even scared myself when I looked into the mirror! No wonder the people in the lobby were looking at me with incredulous stares.

Tim meticulously and gently cleaned off all of the blood, along with little pieces of gritty gravel from the asphalt parking lot. Fortunately, I had liquid Vitamin E with me. The Vitamin E worked wonders in just a few days. I was a little sore for the next several days, with a stiff neck and wounds healing in about eight places on my face. I am used to people staring at me because of my chair, but for several days, people were giving me a different kind of look that focused on the condition of my face and not my wheelchair.

My wheelchair helps me participate with today's fast pace. One of the things that especially touched me was a young person who remembered me from when I visited his school almost two years before. He asked me if my wheelchair still went nine miles per hour. I said yes.

"Cool," he said and smiled.

Writing Tools

"How do you type on the computer?" I am often asked.

I have a small Velcro cuff fitted on my hand. It has a short pencil tucked into it, with the eraser end on the outside. I do the "hunt and peck method," using the eraser end of the pencil to hit the keys. I use the mouse by pushing, pulling and clicking it with the base of my right hand. It is not very fast, but I manage to get the job done. Likewise, I use a similar device, which I attach to my hand. It helps me manually write out checks and greeting cards and things.

Dragon Naturally Speaking for PC's and *Dragon Dictate* for Mac's are two wonderful software packages. They allow the user to verbally put my words to paper, or in this case, onto a computer screen. And what a wonderful tool they are! I highly recommend them to anyone who has trouble using the keyboard for long periods of time. My friend Owen is a master at voice-recognition. He has had a twenty-plus year career working for 3M as a computer programmer without ever touching a mouse. It is fun to watch him maneuver his way around his computer, simply by using voice commands.

While writing, or should I say speaking this book, *Dragon Naturally Speaking* will often times not work properly, because there is something wrong with the microphone. The microphone will need to be unplugged, held for a few seconds, and plugged back in. Then it will work just fine. I cannot do that. If no one is around to perform that simple task, I am not going to write that day. That is very frustrating.

Any problem can be a big problem if it is yours. Do not let anyone tell you what is bothering you is not important. If you think it is a big deal, then it is a big deal and you have to figure it out.

Getting around the house

One day I was giving a presentation at a school built after a tornado had destroyed the previous school. A third grader asked, "What would you do if a tornado came by your house?" I told him I would go into my basement, using the elevator I have in a closet. Once I got in the basement, I would go to the corner of the house facing the direction the tornado was coming from, and hope it did not hit my house.

Young people often ask questions relating to their life experience. The students at that school were all very aware of tornadoes, because the one that destroyed their old school had also destroyed many of their houses. The tornado had a tremendous impact on their lives. They had tornado drills in school and their parents had plans for them at home, should another one come. I get similar questions when speaking after a hurricane, flood, fire or any other disaster.

Another day, while presenting at a school the week after Fire Prevention Week, a little guy raised his hand and wanted to know what I would do if there was a fire in my house. My new house did not have an elevator, so I told him I would go out the back door, down the ramp and away from my house. Then he asked, "What if you couldn't get out the back door?"

"I'd go out the front door and sit on the front step and wait for the fire department to get there."

His hand shot up again and this time he asked, "What if you couldn't get out the front door?"

"I would go in the shower and turn the shower on."

Boom! Up goes his hand again, and this time it was, "Would you take a cold shower?"

I told him I would take a cold shower after my hot water ran out! Guess what? His hand shot up again. "What if there was someone else in the shower?"

I said, "I would tell them, hey, the house is burning down. We'd better get out!"

My little pal was not done. Up went his hand again and he asked, "What if it was a woman?"

At the time, I lived alone. I told him that probably was not very likely to happen. What I noticed about his remarkable line of logical questioning is he was doing exactly what I talk about in my program and asking specific questions. The progression of his line of questioning was very logical and very well thought out. He was thinking, and to me, that was very cool.

Young people need to be able to make sense of things by putting themselves in a particular position. At the beginning of most of my talks, I explain I am a quadriplegic, which means I have lost the function or partial function of all four limbs. Some of the questions I get can be pretty funny. Others show some fairly disturbing things about what is going on in some children's minds. It worries me to see the degree of violence some students find acceptable and even funny. I mentioned earlier I can not feel anything from the middle of my chest down. I tell that to every group and tell them if they scratched, burned, bit or hit my leg, I would not feel it, because the message does not get through my spinal cord and go to my brain. Since the message does not get to the brain, I do not feel the pain.

See, everything starts in your brain. If you wiggle your fingers, it is because your brain sent a message through your spinal cord, down your arm, to your fingers and then your fingers moved. When you walk, your brain tells you to put one foot in front of the other one. If the spinal cord is damaged, the message does not get through, limbs do not work and pain is not felt.

After that description, the hands go up. The questions from some elementary students have shocked me.

"What if I poured acid on your leg, would you feel it?" one student asked.

I answered no and he laughed. "Cool!" he said.

"If I poured gasoline on your legs and then lit them on fire, you wouldn't feel it either?"

"No." And the little guy sat there smiling.

"I would not feel it. But you would be burning my leg, and injuring my skin and muscles," I told him. He sat there, still smiling.

And another child, on another day, asked, "You mean I could cut off your leg with a chain saw, you wouldn't feel it?"

And yet another asked what would happen if she hit my leg with a hammer or pounded a nail in it. The list goes on and gets much worse. Many children have thought it would be cool if they could do those kinds of things to me.

The atmosphere in a group when those kinds of questions start scares me. One question leads to another more horrific question. Think about your curiosity regarding violence and where it comes from. Think about how it affects your life.

In the Community

Over the years, many youth have asked questions about life in a wheelchair. I always tell them I do not like the fact I have to use a wheelchair and how the electronics break down once-in-a-while, or how it gets a flat tire at the worst possible time.

Then I add what I do like is the way I feel about myself now. I mention I do not like the fact some people stare or point at me. I also do not like steps. Nor do I like doorknobs, which I cannot grab onto, because my hands do not work right. But I do like the feeling in my heart and in my head when I can do things without assistance. You see I concentrate on the positive things I can do, not on the negative things I cannot do.

In addition to assistive technology, the Americans with Disabilities Act of 1990 promotes curb cuts and other useful construction for people with and without disabilities.

When children ask me if it is fun being in a wheelchair, I tell them, "No, it is not fun, but I have fun in my chair." I have fun visiting schools and going for walks with a friend, or going to a movie. I have fun taking pictures with my cameras and watching my favorite sport — college basketball. I have had front row seats since 1976, to watch the University of Minnesota's Golden Gophers play basketball. That is what gets me through the Minnesota winters! Special seating, accessible entrances and curb cuts are among the Universal Design features required by the Americans with Disabilities Act of 1990, which help me to be more mobile.

I live in a cool little neighborhood of Minneapolis called Uptown. It is like living in a small town in the middle of a big city. Most days, I can leave my van in the garage and go to all of the important places I need to visit, like the bank and the grocery store (which is also home to my pharmacy). The neighborhood also includes a hardware store. In addition, there are movie theaters and many good restaurants and fast food places for when I need a quick meal. There is even a small shopping mall called Calhoun Square that is close to my house. It has a bookstore, clothing and shoe stores and several restaurants. Plus, Lake Calhoun is only seven blocks from my house. Lake Calhoun makes for a great place to take a walk with friends, including girlfriends.

During my college years, I realized my situation as a quad was going to be long lasting. I started to develop an understanding about my entire body and everything in it. This affected my friendships with males and females alike. As I gained confidence and self-esteem, I learned new ways of thinking about how the world sees me and myself. My being includes physical, spiritual, intellectual and emotional pieces, including sexuality. I came of age in the 70's; of course, dating and relationships would be part of that.

"Maybe I am attractive to the opposite sex, despite all of my physical limitations," I remember thinking when the first girl kissed me after my accident.

Since then, I find the women who have been attracted to me, look beyond my disabilities. They see me as a complete person, including a sexual partner. After college, I attended a couple of Sexual Attitude Readjustment Seminars (SARS) offered through the University of Minnesota. They helped me to learn what was and was not important in a relationship. Still, the sexuality issue continues to be a difficult stepping-stone when I am in on-going relationships.

I know some of my issues seem like they are simple, and they are. The frustration lies in the fact I cannot do anything about them. That is when I feel disabled. It is at those times I have to tell myself, "Don't sweat the small stuff. And, it's all small stuff!"

"The problem isn't the issue – the issue is how you deal with the problem," I say. If I am at a point when my van, wheelchair, body or computer is not cooperating, I remember my own words and just give it up. After all, they are all just "small stuff," I tell every group when I speak.

Chapter Nine

Helping Others Find Meaning

"I'm getting help. It's working too.
THANKS,
I think you saved my life."

Dairy Queen Server
1989

I started speaking to young people in 1975, when Martha Brown, RN, a nursing school instructor asked me to speak to her nursing students about living with a spinal cord injury. I spent three years going to that school once every three weeks to impart my wisdom about life in a wheelchair.

That disability awareness presentation has evolved into a self-esteem presentation that challenges every one of my audience members to reach their potential and to recognize just what their capabilities are. We all have capabilities we do not even know are there. We just have to find them! Sometimes finding our strengths are easy, and other times we go through our whole life and never find them.

One summer evening in 1989, I was in a Dairy Queen with a friend and his two boys, getting a treat after one of his boy's little league baseball games. We were waiting to receive our order when a young lady behind the counter handed me a receipt with a note on the back that read, "I'm getting help. It's working too. Thanks, I think you saved my life."

Then she wrote her name and the high school she attended on that receipt. I looked up in amazement and she was standing behind the counter, smiling and nodding her head up and down! I could not ask her what it was that made her feel that way, because she was very busy, the restaurant was packed, and at just that time our ice cream came, and my friends were leaving the counter to go eat. I shared the note's contents outside the restaurant with my friend. I have wondered about the Dairy Queen girl ever since that evening. By the way, I still have the note. It is framed and sets on a bookshelf in my living room.

I did three presentations on the day I visited her large suburban high school. In the first program, there were one hundred fifty teenagers. In the second, there were maybe three hundred students. After lunch, I came back to the auditorium to find a five hundred-seat room overflowing with about seven hundred young people, many of whom had heard me once or even twice already that day. The aisles were full, the stage had steps all along the front and they were full. People lined the walls. The Fire Marshall would not have approved! The school had more than two thousand students, so they let the teachers choose if they wanted to attend my program or not. The kids heard my program, went to their next class and asked their teachers if they could go hear me again. Word started spreading, and before I knew it, the place was overflowing.

I customize every presentation based on the type of audience. The meeting planners preset goals and objectives, and the event's format. I have to prove myself to each new audience. When I get it just right, it often happens people want to hear my message again.

The Dairy Queen Girl attended one or more of those programs. Each program was different. I do not know what it was I said, but she understood, and it hit her in a way, which prompted her to write, "you saved my life."

Sometimes the seeds we plant come back to us in unexpected ways. As an educator and speaker working with young people, I often hear tragic and depressing stories. It is reassuring when I hear a success story. It is important adults recognize the things we say and do affect children on a daily basis. I believe that holds true for any relationship, no matter the age. One of those situations happened to me, and it took a year to play out.

I was invited to speak at a locked mental health facility for teenagers more than thirty years ago and will never forget it because of what happened after my visit. I went to this locked unit, which was part of a suburban hospital, and I spent ninety minutes with about fifteen teenagers and their staff. We talked about the usual stuff: suicide, depression, drugs, sexuality, hopelessness, parents, relationships, self-esteem, etc. Then I went home.

Two days later, I got a big brown envelope full of letters these teenagers had written to say how they felt after my presentation. One of the letters was from a girl who had not bothered to get dressed the day of my program — there was no reason to get dressed! She showed up in her pajamas and robe. She wrote a two-page letter thanking me for coming and spending time with them. She told me how she had tried to kill herself seven times, and because of my presentation, she would never do it again!

I could not believe what I was reading. I called one of her high school counselors and told him about the letter. He told me more stories about the girl that made me want to cry. The list was long and it included abuse, neglect, alcoholism, anorexia, low self-esteem and much more. The counselor and I discussed the sad state of affairs in the girl's home life.

Little did I know just how much of an affect my presentation, along with the work of two school counselors and the therapy she received in the unit, had accomplished.

About a year later, I went to visit a high school, which happened to be the girl's home school. I was no sooner in the building when this attractive, well-dressed, young woman came running up to me, gave me a big hug, backed up a step or two, held out her arms and said, "Look what you've done. I'm doing great!"

I realized who it was and I said, "I didn't do that. I just gave you some tools; you did everything on your own."

She had literally become a different person. She had changed her name and moved out of the abusive environment where she had been living. She was not sitting under a table in the fetal position in one of the counselor's offices, rocking back and forth for hours at a time anymore. Now, she had a job, a car and an apartment. She was going to college. She was doing very well.

The look on her face at that moment told me she realized for the first time they were her own accomplishments. I believe she was able to take ownership for what she had done and was continuing to do. She seemed to realize a sense of personal responsibility, which enabled her to deal with the situations she had to address. She was doing it. It was a wonderful exchange. I got to spend a short amount of time with her later in the day, and I could not believe this was the same girl who only a year before had come to my presentation in her pajamas!

I found out later the name she took was one of her high school counselor's names. There were a couple counselors in the high school that really made a difference with her, and she said thank you to one of them by taking his surname as her own.

A couple of years later, I spoke with those counselors and they told me the young woman was still in college and seemed to be doing fine. Sure, she had problems, but she appeared to be handling them. She has the tools it will take her to deal with her life situations. She had learned to take personal responsibility for herself. We all need to understand there are people out there who can help us with our problems, people who care. As many of us know, it is not always easy to seek help!

It would be great if we could find out the results of our interactions immediately. Unfortunately, it does not always work that way. Sometimes we need to be patient to see the results of what we say and do with other people. Patience is not always easy, especially with children, but it is important. When young people feel they can trust you, they will tell you just about anything. One day at a conference in Ohio, a girl asked me if she could talk to me in private. I said, "Sure," and we went to a corner of the large ballroom where I had just given the closing keynote speech.

I was astonished from the moment she started talking, and I had a hard time listening to her tragic life story. She told me when she was five; her father started sexually abusing her. She said by the time she was nine; he had her addicted to alcohol and cocaine. She told me if he got out of jail tomorrow, she would kill him! She did not trust her mother, because her mother would not tell her where her brother and sisters were living. She said her foster parents did not trust her. She also told me her social worker rarely came around and when she did, the social worker did not listen to her. She looked at me and said, "All day long people have been telling me they are there for me. They are not there for me. Who is there for me?"

Of all the many stories people have shared with me, this was the saddest.

I told her there might not be anyone for her. I said, "Maybe there is just you and God." I asked her if it would be right to kill her father. She said no, but she would do it anyway; she simply did not care.

I asked her what emotion she felt more than anything, and she said, "Anger."

I asked her if she could turn that anger around and make it become happiness instead. She told me she did not know the answer to my question, because she had never tried to turn it around. She did not know how to be happy! I asked her to smile, which she did and then she said, "Wow, it's been a long time."

Everybody she ever trusted had betrayed her. She did not know what to do. We talked for about twenty minutes before she left – the first time.

It was the end of the day. A few minutes later she came back and wanted to talk some more. She left three more times, but kept coming back. Every time she left, she wanted another hug. These were big-time hugs! It had been quite a while since she had received a hug. The last time she left, she told me she was going to turn that anger around and make it become happiness. Life is all about decisions, and she made a decision that day, which hopefully had a positive effect on the rest of her life.

Two cool things happened that day. One, I had an opportunity to change her perception about her whole life. Two, she trusted me enough to tell me some of her deepest secrets. She told me things she had not told anyone else! She had heard me speak for about an hour, and it is amazing how in that short time period, I had built up enough trust with her so she felt she could tell me anything. We had formed a connection.

I have never heard from her again, and have often wondered how she is doing. I want to believe the connection I made that day planted a seed she has been able to nurture. I may never know, but I hope she is doing well.

According to Dr. Michael Resnick, the director of the University of Minnesota's Healthy Youth Development - Prevention Research Center, "Young people need to feel connected to at least one caring, competent adult. The good news is it doesn't necessarily have to be mom or dad."

I believe the mentorship movement comes from that need for the connectedness young people have with adults. As you know, many young people grow up today in households with little or no supervision, single parents with little or no time for their children, and dysfunctional two-parent families that provide bad role models. They are exposed to excessive amounts of graphic violence on television, in movies and video games. All of these things lead to a lack of connectedness. Many young people feel more connected to their video games and cable television than they do to their parents.

"School is nothing more than practice," I tell students. "School is practice for life after school. It is practice for life. If you have ever been on a sports team, I am willing to bet your coach has said, you will play like you practice."

If you believe you will play like you practice, then you need to build relationships based on trust. We hear people talk about "quality time." I do not believe it is quality time as much as it is about quantity of time. Any amount of time has potential to be quality time.

On August 24, 1994, I spent four hours with about two-dozen wonderful teenage volunteers at Minneapolis Children's Medical Center. Margaret O'Connor was the Junior Volunteer Coordinator at MCMC. She asked me to spend time helping her recognize these young people for volunteering for as many as five hundred hours! The youth were as young as thirteen years old. They had just finished the summer program. Some of these young people had been volunteering for as long as three and four years! They came from schools in Minneapolis and from several suburbs. One girl, who lived forty-five minutes away, received recognition for volunteering more than three hundred hours.

At one point, I said something to the effect about them not being paid.

"But we are being paid, just not with money," one of the girls said.

The payment she was referring to involved the hugs, smiles, pats on the back, verbal "thank yous" and the kisses the patients and staff at the hospital were giving to them every day. These volunteers were giving the greatest gift they could give, the gift of themselves. They received rewards all the time. It appeared to this first-timer the hugs Margaret and her staff were generously handing out, along with smiles and thank you comments were more than ample compensation for this tremendous group of young volunteers. There is a real sense of warmth and caring in this program. The atmosphere starts with adults and rubs off on young people. The program is a great example of how things adults say and do affect youth.

"Students need to hear the good stuff more than once," a teacher once told me. I agree. They need to hear it from parents, teachers, mentors, me and any other adults who play a part in their lives. If young people hear the good stuff time and time again, hopefully, eventually it will sink in. The thing is, we may never know the effect we have produced at the time. Many young people will not share with adults what you are telling them makes sense—unless they trust you. Even if they trust you, chances are good, they are not going to share the effect you have had on them with you.

On the other hand, many times students want to tell me their stories — right after my speech. On occasion, tragic stories have led me to contact a school counselor to see if there was help available. When others share the message of hope and inspiration they heard from me has changed them, I am ecstatic! I have often said, "There is a reason why I got hurt." I am constantly reminded of that statement. In fact, I believe there are several reasons why I got hurt and why I am still here.

For instance, I hope by hearing the stories I share, nursing and other medical career students understand the importance of their words and non-verbal communications with their patients. School personnel can make a huge difference and impact their students' lives. The same is true for medical professionals and their patients.

In fact, communication is the key for all relationships, whether they take place at home, work or in the community. Since ninety-three percent of communication is non-verbal, we need to be aware of our body language, facial expressions, how we interact, and how we share our accomplishments and failures with others.

Chapter Ten

Reaching Persons with Disabilities

"I don't know if you'll remember me or not; but I was the girl with the shiny silver walker in the front row of your presentation … I was just writing to say thanks. You see, I have a condition called cerebral palsy that I was born with and I've had to deal with the problems of being disabled all my life. Lately-because of high school-it's been really hard to deal, and some of the things that you mentioned really hit home. I was so moved that I was brought to tears. For a couple minutes there, I was incredibly close to just breaking down and bawling. I know that our situations are pretty different; but some of the things that I've experienced when it comes to how people react to me are a lot alike-the patronizing and everything. I've never met anyone who's openly talked about that whose had to really deal with it; and hearing you talk about it lifted a lot of weight off my shoulders. Realizing that I wasn't the only one felt so awesome! I cried again. And then when you got to the part where you talked about your friends not noticing your wheelchair anymore, I totally lost it. I practically had tears streaming down my face. You see, I got ditched by my friends last year and have been feeling really insecure ever since. All I want is for people to see me and not my disability; and when I heard that you had accomplished that, it gave me such tremendous hope. You have no idea how glorious that feels. Thank you so much. You're such an inspiration to me. All the odds were against you and you rose above them. I only hope that I can do half as well as you have. Thank you for your time."

Melanie Ann Larson, Freshman

"Of course, I remember you," I responded to Melanie. I agreed there was hope as she was beginning to build her life's foundation. When I received her email, it had been twenty-eight years since I got hurt. I asked her to be patient. I shared that there were people she could talk to (including me), and I affirmed she was a bright young woman for whom life would unfold. "Just try and enjoy being a freshman now," I added.

I have given two types of presentations to impart my wisdom about life in a wheelchair. They include a disability awareness presentation for medical professionals and a self-esteem presentation. The second presentation challenges every audience member to reach their potential and to recognize just what their capabilities are. We all have capabilities, which we do not even know are there. We just have to find them!

Sometimes finding our strengths are easy, and other times we go through our whole lives and never find them. Personally, I am always exploring new ways to address the issues I deal with, like writing this book and keeping my blog updated. Everywhere I go unbelievable things happen. I meet amazing people like the student with cerebral palsy who took the time to reach out by sending a thank you note to me.

One of my favorite annual events is the Virginia Youth Leadership Forum. Nothing I know of compares to what happens during the week I spend with a small group of individuals at the Virginia Youth Leadership Forum (VYLF). Each year, the program director, Teri Barker, brings in twenty to twenty-five students who will be entering their junior or senior year of high school in the fall. All of the students have disabilities of one sort or another; some of them are severely disabled and medically fragile. The forum has a nurse on staff, and five or six personal care attendants are available at all times to help young people who may need assistance.

Besides the students with disabilities, Teri also has a staff consisting of former delegates, many of whom have been involved with the program since its inception. Everyone has his or her assignments. From my perspective, the program appears to run very smoothly. However, if one were to ask some of the staff members how well the program runs, they may get a completely different answer, especially after a staff member has just put out a small fire!

One of the staff members, Thomas, has been at all five of the programs I have attended. He uses a three-wheel scooter to get around, because he is significantly affected by cerebral palsy. He has tight muscle spasms and a severe speech disability. He also has a smile that lights up the room! He and I became fast friends, and we have made each other laugh more times than I can count. When there is a low point, all I have to do is look his way, catch his eyes, and we both start smiling. Thomas does not need to develop character because he already is one!

At the 2005 Virginia YLF, I met another young staff member by the name of Matt Deans. Matt had been in a car accident a few years earlier. He broke his back in the lower thoracic region and became an extremely high functioning paraplegic. Matt has an incomplete injury, which allows him to perform several daily-living activities. For instance, in 2005, he was getting around by using crutches.

The Monday night after my opening keynote address, Matt, Tim, one or two other people and I were sitting outside the dorm talking. We were discussing Matt's gait and how difficult it was on his knees. Because of the limited muscle function and dramatic atrophy he has in his legs, walking puts tremendous pressure on his knees. He responded to my comments.

"No disrespect intended Sir, but by the time I get to be your age I'll probably have to have my knees replaced," he said to me in a very respectful way.

I chuckled, and replied, "No disrespect taken."

At the time, I was fifty years old and almost thirty-four years post injury. Matt was all of twenty-three! I am not sure exactly how long post injury Matt was, but with the very polite, gentleman-like manner in which he made his "no disrespect intended" comment, I definitely knew I was in the South!

During my speech at the mentoring luncheon, I mentioned how tired I was, because Matt had kept me up until 1:00 a.m. the night before. I told them I was just getting too old to do that anymore.

"But I couldn't leave, because you wouldn't stop talking," Matt yelled out from his seat towards the back of the ballroom.

It was a great comment! It drew a resounding laugh from the audience and a "Touché," from me. It is unscripted moments like that, which often leave an indelible memory to cherish.

Matt, Teri and the rest of the staff are there mainly for the students, but they help speakers out too. For instance, during my third year speaking at YLF, my attendant Tim and I arrived to see Teri, as usual, waiting to greet us. Tim got out of the van, and he greeted Teri while the driver of the lift-equipped van unlocked my chair and began to get me off the bus. Then, I started connecting with staff members who I had met in previous years. There are many very special people involved in this YLF program, and I feel privileged to have the opportunity to know them.

One more note about Matt and his wife, Ashley. By the time you are reading this, they will be parents for the first. I am very happy for them and they are excited for the opportunity to be parents. I wish them well.

Other leadership programs last from Friday afternoon until Sunday afternoon. A lot also happens in these shorter forums with young leaders, with and without disabilities. The programs may include groups of up to three hundred or more high school students! I watch youth come from all parts of a state or region of the country. They may not know anyone else at the event, but by the time just two short days have gone by, they make relationships that may last a lifetime. When put in an excellent learning environment, these young people, who are surrounded by positive, like-minded individuals, grow and develop in ways that are absolutely amazing!

One night at the Virginia YLF, four groups each put on skits. Their theme was "Learn, Empower, Achieve, Demonstrate — LEAD." Each group had to work from a scenario and give their version of how that scenario would play out.

Now remember, only two days earlier these young people had shown up on campus knowing no one.

Many were very shy and most had never been on stage! All of them gave excellent short skits that brought the house down!

One young man, Steven, has severe cerebral palsy involvement. He uses a wheelchair to get around and a talking board to communicate. That night he stole the show. At the end of the skit, he managed to stand up and flex his arms over his head in a classic bodybuilder pose. The smile on his face went from ear to ear! As a matter-of-fact, he did the pose several times. He did not want to get off the stage!

In just forty-eight hours, these teens go from being quiet, shy and almost bashful individuals to being expressive, cohesive teams. They perform on stage in what can only be described as heartwarming events.

Part of their week on campus is devoted to group activity time, where they work on a five-year plan. In other words, where do they want to be in five years and how are they going to get there. I have seen some very well done paths to reach their goals, created with much thought and creativity.

Teri provides delegates with plenty of art materials and a well-put-together manual. Leadership teams then help the delegates create effective, fun and very useful paths for their futures.

Virginia YLF culminates in students who have special needs, giving presentations before members of the Virginia legislature! I have never seen anything like it. When the students arrive on Monday, legislators, parents and staff greet them with cheers, applause, hugs and high-fives. The delegates often tell people the legislature presentation is one of the highlights of their leadership experience.

One year as my personal assistant Tim and I left campus to catch our flight back to Minneapolis, students were boarding buses for their trip to the State Capitol building in Richmond. They were going to give their testimonies for a panel of Virginia government officials, including legislators from the Virginia Assembly and Senate. They also got a group picture taken with the Governor.

Prior to the Capitol visit, I brought two students who had asked me to read their testimonies onto the stage. Jacqueline and Taylor had picked excellent topics, and they were prepared to give fine testimonies to the legislature. Because of their willingness to ask me to read their testimonies and their willingness to show leadership, I wanted to reward them with a book titled, *LEAD Now or Step Aside.* I did not write the book, but I did write a chapter in it.

Because Jacqueline and Taylor had been the first to ask me to read their testimonies, I decided I would give them not only the book, but an ATTITUDE pin as well. I give an ATTITUDE pin to one or more audience members at the end of every presentation in a little game I play with someone who has demonstrated something during my speech that tells me they are worthy of a special gift.

Before I gave Jacqueline and Taylor their ATTITUDE pins, I grabbed my briefcase and told them I had something else I wanted to give them, but they had to promise me they would wear it every day for the rest of their lives!

They smiled very uneasy smiles for a bit, contemplated my proposition, and not quite sure what was going on, both of them hesitantly nodded their heads and said they would wear what I wanted to give them.

While they were contemplating my offer, I could see they were not quite sure what was going on.

"What's wrong, don't you trust me? Do you think I would do something to make you uncomfortable or embarrassed?" I asked them.

While this was happening, I was opening a compartment in my briefcase where I keep my pins. I asked Jacqueline to please reach into my briefcase and grab two of the little plastic bags. She reached into the briefcase and grabbed several bags.

"I said two bags, not all of them," I told her in a joking manner.

She took two bags and gave one of them to Taylor. Then she started to examine just what was in her plastic bag. I told Jacqueline and Taylor they had to wear these pins to make them work.

"Attitude is everything," I told them.

Then I asked Jacqueline, Taylor and the rest of the audience if they had ever seen the phrase, "Attitude is everything." I put the word ATTITUDE on the screen behind me. It showed a list I had received from a student after an assembly in a high school in Wisconsin a few years before.

The word ATTITUDE had a number beneath each of its letters. The numbers corresponded to their position in the alphabet.

A was the number 1
T was the number 20
T again was the number 20
I was the number 9
T was the number 20
U was the number 21
D was the number 4
E was the number 5.

By the way, if you add all the numbers together, their total is 100. I like that.

I find it an amazing coincidence how, when you put the previous paragraph into perspective, attitude truly is everything. I find myself referring to that phrase all the time.

I buy ATTITUDE pins by the hundreds, and I give them out on a daily basis. I have often run into someone at a later date to whom I have given a pin, and they are wearing their ATTITUDE pin. They are always quick to point out they are wearing their pins. I love it! I have a page on the Materials page of my website which reads, "Attitude is Everything." Feel free to click on it and print it for your bulletin board.

There are days when I have given my pin to someone for any one of a number of reasons, and I will make some smart comment like, "That's okay, it needed adjusting anyway." Or I will say, "Don't worry, I'll find another attitude."

Just remember, it is all about your ATTITUDE!

Chapter Eleven

Problem Solving Through Role Playing

This was sent to the Minneapolis StarTribune after an article appeared in the paper about me on the fortieth anniversary of my accident, September 3, 2011: *"Greetings – I was hoping you could get a message to Mike Patrick – he was our coach in the 1970's at Flip Saunders Summer Basketball Camp in Golden Valley. Mike taught us how to play Backgammon, not to mention basketball. Our Mom was raising my brother and me by herself and was at work. Mike and Flip did a fantastic job of looking after us. We loved those guys. Mike was really our main coach there. We will NEVER forget them. We were just kids. The article and photo of Mike are a real treat after all these years!!! His impact on kids resonates over decades, miles and memories. Thank you, Mike!!"*

Stacy L. Hutchens
Probation Officer
Marion County Superior Courts
Indianapolis, IN
September 6, 2011

Too many times, we compare our problems to those of other people. I do not believe we should do that. We see problems on the news, hear about them on the radio and read about them in newspapers, books, and magazines as well as on the Internet. I believe very strongly we cannot compare our problems to someone else's! It is human nature to compare our lives to others' lives. I still do that sometimes, and when I do, I have to stop and remember my own advice.

Comparisons are not a healthy way to address your issues. This holds true for anyone, no matter how old you are, or whether your issues involve chronic illness and disability like me, or you are facing financial problems, or other life-changing events and decisions. Almost every day, medical and teaching professionals have opportunities to help patients and students open their eyes to new possibilities when they have difficult choices and decisions to make. When I am confronted with an issue, I often hear myself saying, "Remember Mike, the problem isn't the issue, the issue is how you deal with problem."

My favorite exercise for looking at options is "Stuck in the Desert." It has provided many incredible experiences during the hundreds of times I have conducted it with all ages of people. It encourages people to look within themselves and see how they solve problems, to find out what their priorities are.

I will present the exercise first. Then I will share several stories that have happened during presentations, and you will see if you can learn anything about yourself. So, grab a pen or pencil and a piece of paper. Once you read the problem, do the exercise BEFORE you read the rest of this chapter. You must know, there are no right or wrong answers. This is all about you. It is about you and your feelings. It is about how you see the world. It is about how you solve problems. Once you see your own methodology, you may be able to see how others solve their problems and help them to either accept their decisions or look at other options.

3444344

Stuck In The Desert:

You are in a desert and you have no idea where you are. You have with you the following five animals:
Lion
Monkey
Sheep
Cow
Horse

To escape the desert you are going to have to get rid of one of your animals. Which one do you drop? Why do you drop it? Write your answer down, because you will refer to it later. You may use whatever logic you like, BUT keep track of which animal you discard and when and why you discard it! Remember, this is all about you. It is your desert and your decision about what that means.

You have four animals left. The desert is burning up! It goes on for miles. Sand is everywhere. You realize to get out; you are going to have to drop another animal. Which one do you drop and why?

You have three animals left. You walk and walk. It is getting hotter and hotter and, "Oh no," it is a disaster! The oasis you were looking for is dried up! You have no choice but to drop another animal.

You have two animals left. Okay, it is a long, hot walk. You can see the edge of the desert far away on the horizon. Unfortunately, you can only leave the desert with ONE animal. Which animal do you drop, and which one do you keep and why?

If you are doing this in a class as a group exercise, before discussing the answers, make sure you know which animal you dropped and in what order. I have initiated great discussions about this exercise; some of which have lasted up to an hour. The following answers are based on Japanese Archetypes, which are original models after which other similar problems are patterned.

1st animal dropped and why

2nd animal dropped and why

3rd animal dropped and why

4th animal dropped and why

5th animal kept and why

At this point, I ask for participants who would like to share their answers. Usually, I get more people who want to share her or his response than we have time to discuss. It always makes for great conversations. I want to share a few responses with you and tell you how I answered the problem.

Personal and Community Resource Program

On May 7, 1998, I spent two hours at a church in a Minneapolis suburb with Mary Jane Hackett and thirty women who were preparing to do volunteer work with a group in the Personal and Community Resource Program.

I had several responses, and most of the participants were keeping their monkey. In fact, twenty-seven of the thirty women took the monkey out of the desert with them. That large of a percentage for keeping the monkey was unusually high. They gave many reasons like:

"I could play with it because it is the most intelligent of all the animals."

"I could nurture and protect it."

"I could talk to it."

"I could teach it sign language and communicate with it that way."

"If we found a palm tree, it could climb the tree and get a coconut."

"It could entertain me."

They gave me many of the reasons why moms have children. It was fun to see.

Almost immediately after, I explained what all the pieces of the exercise represented. The three women who did not take the monkey out of the desert, practically in unison replied, "Does that mean I am a bad parent?"

I said, "I doubt it. Are your children grown, and have they moved away from home?"

They all said, "Yes, their children were grown and had moved away from home."

Then, I confidently said, "I'm not even going to ask, you all rode your horse out of the desert. Tell me I am wrong."

All three said, yes they rode out of the desert on their horse.

I told them their children were grown and probably did not need their nurturing any more. They all agreed and everyone had a good laugh.

Watching Stuck In the Desert Play Out

I was in Lawrence, Kansas on January 24, 1999, to present the opening keynote address for the Kansas Recreation and Parks Association Annual Conference the next day. Through several emails back and forth between their director, Laura Kelly and me, she arranged for me to attend a Kansas University basketball game at the famous Allen Field House. It is one of the all-time great venues to watch big-time college basketball.

Laura's assistant, Annette Deghand and her husband, Scott, had borrowed a van much like mine to transport my attendant and me from the airport in Kansas City, to the hotel in Lawrence, and then back to Kansas City. They also used it to take my friend, Lew Ruona and me to watch the game between KU and Missouri that Sunday afternoon.

When we arrived at the field house, Annette and Scott dropped Lew and me off in a parking lot and told us they would pick us up there after the game. Then, they went and parked the van in another lot.

We had courtside seats, and we had a great time watching my favorite sport in one of the most storied arenas in the country. Little did I know as we left the field house the game would not be the highlight of my day.

We ran into Annette and Scott in the lobby and walked out together with them. When we got out of the building, Scott went to get the van and Annette came with us to talk about the game and wait for Scott. That was about 3:00 p.m.

With more than fourteen thousand people trying to leave campus at once, there were cars everywhere. Campus Police were directing traffic and clearing all of the parking lots. They were slowly emptying. At about 3:30 p.m., a police car complete with lights flashing and sirens screaming was slowly trying to come against the outgoing traffic.

Annette's reaction was, "Oh no! Scott's been in an accident!"

I assured her the police car had nothing to do with Scott.

Not two minutes later, here came an ambulance, again with lights flashing and sirens screaming. Once again, Annette started to get scared. She said Scott had never driven that van. A friend had lent it to the agency to cart me around for a few days. Scott was not listed as one of the insured drivers and she had a bad feeling.

"What does Scott do for a living?" I asked.

She said he was a firefighter, and lately they had not had any calls to fires. Instead, they had calls to several accidents, and she was afraid this time Scott was in an accident. We continued to wait for Scott, and at 3:45 p.m., he still had not shown up. The traffic police were already gone, the barricades were gone, and we were the only people left in the parking lot. About ten minutes later, Scott finally pulled into our lot.

When he got out of the van, his face was very pale and he started apologizing right away. He said he was so sorry for being late, but he had been holding a kid's head in his hands, and he was not sure if the young man was going to make it.

"There is no reason to apologize," I told him and then asked, "What happened?"

I am paraphrasing, but this is essentially what he said. He told us he was waiting behind one car at a four-way stop, and the car to his left pulled into the intersection. As the car in front of him pulled out, the second car to his left decided he was going to go as well. He T-boned the car in front of Scott and smashed the car with a direct hit!

The back window was smashed. Scott said he could see how the driver was unconscious, because he was not moving and his head was tipped back. He told us he shoved his own van into Park, turned it off and jumped out. He went into the person's car through their back window. He tried to stabilize the young man's head until they could "board him." (He was referring to getting the young man on a body board to stabilize the spine because of a potential spinal cord injury.) He told us he held the student's head for a good thirty minutes before they got him out of the car.

Then, he checked his person to see if he had any glass shards on his body. He also checked to see if he had any blood on his clothes or was bleeding anywhere. Scott was just coming down from his adrenaline rush!

I was AMAZED! As Scott was telling his account of his actions, I started thinking about how he had just done *Stuck In The Desert*! First of all, he left his pride in his van when he jumped out of it. His passion for saving lives kicked in. He did not worry about his children because they were safe with the babysitter at their house. He was worried about his wife and friends, but his passion for saving lives was much stronger. He apologized over and over again to us because of what he had to do.

Finally, Scott's basic needs were set on the back burner when he disregarded his own needs and went through the jagged edges of glass around the back window and maneuvered through the glass, which was all over the back seat. It was not until he came down from his adrenaline rush that he thought about his own basic needs.

The day started out ordinary, but then Scott's experience and its close parallel to *Stuck in the Desert* left an indelible mark on me. I am glad I got to witness *Stuck in the Desert* play out so vividly. However, I hope never to experience it in such a manner ever again.

Hubert H. Humphrey Job Corps

On April 18, 2002, I was at the Hubert H. Humphrey Job Corps in St. Paul, Minnesota. I did an assembly for the entire student body, and then I presented three small-group sessions. In the last session, Lenny, from inner city Cincinnati, told me about his solution to the exercise.

The first thing he would do is kill the monkey and feed it to the lion, because he wanted to take care of the lion, so the lion would be his friend and protect him. Then, he said he would kill the sheep for the same reason. By this time, most of the other students were shocked, and others laughed. I told them to hang on and let him finish. There was something extraordinary going on here.

The next thing Lenny said he would do was milk the cow for the last time. Then he would kill it, butcher it and take enough meat to sustain him for a short time. After that, he would let the lion feed on the carcass, and he would ride out of the desert on the horse.

Lenny said, "Once the lion realized I was gone, he would track me and follow me out of the desert. When I got out of the desert, I would have the horse to ride and the lion to protect me."

It was COOL! Lenny was demonstrating abstract thinking skills, which many adults do not possess. It is definitely not a part of most normal adolescent development. I told the students who had been laughing and mocking Lenny he was actually showing some extraordinary skills, which many people do not have.

I asked Lenny if anyone had ever told him he had leadership potential and skills.

"No, nobody has ever told me that," Lenny said.

I told him he had just shown leadership potential by demonstrating abstract thinking in a critical thinking exercise. You could see him sit up straighter as I said that. I hope he is doing well.

Agriculture Class In Marengo, Iowa

On February 25, 2003, I was in Marengo, Iowa speaking to a small group of students in an agriculture class. Most of these students lived on farms near this small town in east central Iowa.

We did the *Stuck In The Desert* exercise and one young man started to give me his answer. Almost verbatim, he was giving me the answers Lenny had given me. I was shocked! What is going on here? How could a white student who lives on a farm in Iowa be thinking the same way as a black youth from inner city Cincinnati?

Talk about two people coming from very different backgrounds and very different experiences; in my mind, they could not be any more different. What I came to believe from that experience is the Japanese Archetype of the participants in this exercise holds true, despite their coming from different environments. We are more alike than we are different.

St. Cloud Technical High School

On September 12, 2005, I was speaking to the student body of about thirteen hundred students and staff in the gymnasium at St. Cloud Technical High School in St. Cloud, Minnesota. I was completely drenched from a hard rain, which caught me while I was getting from my van into the building. My day had not started out very well!

After my ninety-minute assembly and a standing ovation, I was drying off and feeling much better. I spent the rest of the day in their auditorium presenting six small group programs. I love busy days like that. When I do a day with multiple small group sessions, or as I call them — classroom visits, I try to do each one a little differently. I have so much material; no matter how long I spend with a group I always drive home thinking of things I wish I had said.

We did the *Stuck In The Desert* exercise in one of the sessions, and something happened that had never happened before or since.

When I started asking for volunteers to share their answers, one young lady raised her hand and said, "The first thing I did was write a word after each animal, which I thought represented what the animal meant to me."

This is what she had written:

> Lion — protection
> Monkey — friend
> Sheep — heat
> Cow — milk
> Horse — ride

Then, she told me she prioritized dropping her animals by what they could do for her. She said the first thing she dropped was the sheep because it represented heat to her and she was in the desert, so she did not need any more heat.

The next animal she dropped was the monkey, because she did not need a friend. Next was the cow because by this time, it would not give milk any more. The fourth animal to go was the horse, because she could see the edge of the desert and she figured she could walk that far. What she needed was protection once she got out of the desert.

I did not ask why she needed protection. I wish I would have. I often wonder what her reasoning was.

The Way I Got Out Of The Desert

When I first did this exercise, the animals were not presented in the order I gave them to you. The reason I listed the animals at the beginning of this chapter in a specific order is it is the order in which I dropped the animals.

Now, I know what problem I was addressing and why I solved my problem the way I did. I was thinking about my accident! I dropped my lion first because my pride went right out the window after my first or second bed bath when I knew what the nurse was doing, and I could not feel anything. I had to simply lie there, naked, completely exposed to the world and feeling very vulnerable.

The monkey went next because I did not have any children. I was a child myself. And my parents would take care of my younger siblings.

Then I dropped the sheep, because although I was getting friends coming to visit virtually every day and/or evening, there was no one there at 3:00 a.m. when I was crying myself to sleep, feeling sorry for myself.

Then, I had a choice between the cow and the horse, and I gave up the cow because I needed the horse to ride out. My basic needs were obviously not met when I lost forty percent of my body weight in that first hospital!

At that point, my passion was to stay alive. I know what my passion is now. My passion is speaking. I love the idea of having opportunities to change and improve lives every time I speak. I did not know that when I was sixteen. I know now. It has taken a long journey to get where I am, and the major reason I have made it this far has been my passion. I am passionate about everything I do. It is not easy, but it is what drives me.

As Ralph Waldo Emerson said, "Nothing great was ever achieved without passion."

By now, I am sure you want to know what everything represents if you have not figured it out from Scott's story or my response. When I present, I save this part for the end — after people have had a chance to tell me what they did. Again, they tell me all sorts of things. The stories I have shared here have stuck out and shown me how different people would respond to a hardship.

This is what the desert and the animals represent:

The desert represents a hardship. I believe hardship is simply another word for problem.

> Lion — pride
> Monkey — children
> Sheep — friendship
> Cow — basic needs
> Horse — passion

Remember, there are no right or wrong answers. Does any of this make sense to you? Do the results you received coincide with your belief system? If they do, what do you believe they mean? Does the way you did this exercise tell you anything about your strengths and weaknesses? Does it tell you anything about your strengths and weaknesses, which you can work on?

I have put the ball in your court. Now, it is your chance to decide if you want to play. I REALLY like this exercise!

Chapter Twelve

Keys to Overcoming Adversity

"Perhaps with the right equipment, Mike, you could drive."

Driver's Training Instructor

Although the adversity I have had to overcome has been monumental, I ask others not to minimize their problems by comparing them to mine — or to anyone else's, for that matter.

"Don't worry, it's really no big deal," someone might say to another person who confides in them. Well, if something is going on, and it feels like a problem, it is a problem! Yes, looking back on it a few weeks, months, or years later, it really may not have been such a big deal. But this is not the future, it is now. And now, it is a problem!

My years of overcoming adversity have also given me years of positive, problem-solving experiences and opportunities. Besides having a positive attitude, it is also important to take time to learn to use a process to overcome adversity.

Four Keys To Overcoming Adversity

I believe there are four primary keys to overcoming adversity. They are desire, motivation, persistence and flexibility. Obviously, these are not the only factors that determine whether one will succeed, but if they are not present, success is unlikely.

Before we look at how these factors affect success, I want to remind you again — never underestimate your capabilities. While I was still in the hospital after my injury, one of my doctors called my family out of my room, took them to the waiting room and told them I would never drive a car, never own a home, never work, never sit up straight in a wheelchair, or never get married. He gave me a rather grim prognosis!

Key #1: Desire

To overcome adversity, you need to have the desire to solve the problem. This may seem rather obvious, but think about it. If you do not want to do something, it is not going to happen! Earlier, I mentioned my friend Ed Roberts who co-founded the World Institute on Disability. He was a quad who contracted polio as a teenager; subsequently, he used a ventilator and an iron lung. Ed had the desire to go to college, and practically had to fight his way in when told, "We've tried cripples and they don't work." Not only did Ed attend college, he was also a founder of the Berkeley Disabled Students Program, a leader of the nation's first Center for Independent Living, and a lifelong civil rights activist. His desire paved the way for me – and others like me – to attend college and live independently. I bought my first house when I was twenty-three and still live in my own home. Despite one doctor's prognosis, I can sit up in my chair. I just need to use a back brace, because I also have a broken back. I am not married, but I have had girlfriends. What is it you desire to overcome?

Key #2: Motivation

Once you have the desire to accomplish a task, you need the drive, the incentive and the motivation to do so. Thomas Edison, who was hard-of-hearing, invented the phonograph, the Projectoscope (for motion pictures) and many other communication devices. Edison was so motivated he had over 1,000 patents.

Dr. Leon Sullivan, the Baptist minister I mentioned in an early chapter, faced racial discrimination as a youth. His desire to change the system helped produce thousands of jobs for African Americans and other disenfranchised groups. Dr. Sullivan organized boycotts, more than twenty self-help programs and created his own Principals of Social Responsibility, which are still in use by global companies. Dr. Sullivan was motivated by an incident that occurred at the age of twelve and went on to become a very effective leader of the Civil Rights movement.

Dr. Sullivan motivated me toward my own self-help activities and to serving others. Looking at one my own late teenage experiences, I realized being able to drive would not only give me a great deal of freedom and mobility, it would also open up many opportunities. I once tried to drive a car with hand controls, but found it impossible. Fortunately, the driver's training instructor with whom I worked had a positive attitude, and he motivated me to learn how to drive a van.

"Perhaps with the right equipment, Mike, you could drive," the instructor told me.

What or who motivates you to work harder to overcome a situation?

Key #3: Persistence

Solving a problem requires persistence. You have to

keep working at it. Do not give up at the first sign of failure — or the second, or third, or fourth or fifth. Be persistent. Anne Sullivan, who was Helen Keller's teacher, was vision impaired herself and was left in an orphanage as a young child. Yet, she had persistence, and she wanted an education despite her disability and station in life. Her persistence eventually led her to spend several years teaching one of the worlds' most famous deaf and blind persons how to communicate.

Being persistent may not always lead to greatness, but I would like to know what happened to the tornado-surviving, third-grader who would not stop asking questions about how I would escape a fire. The progression of his line of questioning was very logical and very well thought out. He was thinking, and to me, that was very cool.

Likewise, persistence has helped me to overcome adversity. For example, after the doctor told my family I would never be able to drive, my driver's training instructor told me maybe I could drive with the right equipment. He gave me the name of a medical equipment company. After following up with them, I found a California-based dealer who sold adapted vans, which I could drive from my wheelchair. The van had controls that could be adapted to my needs and abilities. Even after I had the vehicle, more adjustments were necessary before everything worked correctly. As a result of persistence, I am now on my sixth van and have driven nearly one-half million miles. I often drive the van to speaking engagements.

Persistence was also involved in my career choice. I had to try several different positions, until I found something that fit me. This persistence eventually led to motivational speaking. Had I listened to the doctor with the grim prognosis, I might never have tried to work at all — or I might have tried one or two jobs and then given up. I may never have lived to hear the youth say to me, "Cuz, you're not done yet."

Is there a situation in your life that deserves your persistence in giving it one more try?

Key #4: Flexibility

There is no point in being persistent if you are just going to repeat the first solution you came up with again and again. If Plan A does not work, try Plan B. If that does not work, go to Plan C. Try to take different approaches to your problem. Keep trying until you have success. A good strategy is to divide a problem into smaller pieces and work on each one separately. For example, let's say you move to a new city and do not know anyone. You feel alone aside from a few work colleagues, and you do not really know what to do about forming new friendships. How can you accomplish this? It is unlikely you could find ten or fifteen new friends in a short time, but you could find one. So you might begin by setting a goal to find one person in the next week you could eat lunch with. Then, during the following week or two, try to find another person. As you get to know one or two people, through them you will meet more. Eventually, you will have a new group of friends.

My friend Jody, who when diagnosed with pancreatic cancer and given six to nine months to live, was flexible. Her flexibility, desire and motivation to live, along with her persistence to beat one of the most-mortal cancers, helped her to beat her prognosis by over seven months. She had an attitude of simply dealing with the big stuff. She credited me for that attitude, but Jody was a trooper through the whole process.

When I broke my neck, the challenge of living with my disability seemed hopeless. Everything that was important to me was suddenly taken away. My problems felt insurmountable. Everything I liked to do, I did with my arms and legs, but I could not move them anymore. Eventually, my attitude changed, and I was able, one-step at a time, to begin creating a new life for myself.

Having the freedom of mobility beyond my wheelchair was one way I could create a new life. When I first tried to drive and failed, I thought I would never drive again, because I was only thinking about driving a regular car. It had not occurred to me someone might be able to adapt a car or van to meet my needs — until my driver-training instructor mentioned this as a possibility.

Think more about the last key to success. Being flexible also requires us to be open to new ideas and unforeseen situations and solutions. Sometimes a solution is right at hand, but we just do not recognize it ... or if we do, we do not want to accept it.

Sometimes when the solution arrives, you will have to change your perception and be willing to say, "Oh! That is the direction I need to go."

My career is another example of changing my perception of a situation. I tried a number of different jobs before settling into public speaking, and I actually tried a number of speaking jobs before settling into what I now do. I had the desire to work. I had the motivation to look for work. I had persistence to keep looking and trying. Finally, I had the flexibility to try different positions until I found something perfectly fit for me.

Had I listened to that doctor, I might never have tried to work at all — or I might have tried only one or two jobs and then given up when they did not work out. I love my work today, but I did not know what I had been missing until it arrived.

I could have seen my various "failed" attempts at working as just that — failures. What we call "failure" however, may not be failure. Try thinking about failures as markers pointing you in new directions. Eventually, there is a solution, one, which might never have been found without the failures. I know part of my purpose in life is to change peoples' lives, to help all who read this to know you too are not done yet.

When dealing with adversity, be flexible. Be persistent. Open your mind to as many possibilities as you can. Be creative. Like me, you will be amazed with the outcome. I am not done yet. I hope you are not done yet, either.

Henry Ford once said, "Whether you think you can or whether you think you can't — you're right!"

What can help you be persistent in the goal of doing what you believe you can or cannot do? In other words, how are you not done yet?

To continue the discussion in this book, please visit and subscribe to my blog, I Am Not Done Yet (iamnotdoneyet.blogspot.com).

CPSIA information can be obtained at www.ICGtesting.com
Printed in the USA
LVOW12s1247230415

435777LV00003B/4/P